The Nazi UFOs Where Are They Now?

Mohamed Cherif

Published by Mohamed Cherif, 2022.

THE NAZI UFOS WHERE ARE THEY NOW?

First edition. August 24, 2022.

ISBN: 979-8201430900

Written by Mohamed Cherif.

Table of Contents

C.1: Admiral Richard Byrd and Nazis UFOs

After the World War II, between August 1946 and February 1947, the USA sent an expedition fleet for Antarctica for multiple purposes including the settling there .The header of this convoy was Admiral Richard Byrd who was graduated from the United States Naval Academy in Annapolis, fought in WWI then became an explorer. In 1926, he was the first one who fly over the North Pole with pilot Floyd Bennett both received the congressional medal of honor .In the age of 41, he conducted the expedition to Antarctica.

The expedition crew was formed by 4700 members spread in 13 ships including Icebreakers, Supply ships, Tankers, Destroyer, Submarine and Aircrafts Carrier and a total number of 33 aircrafts and Helicopters! So, it can be considered as a small army! Anyone can reacts by asking is all that for a simple expedition?

Every team was concerned to discover a specified area of Antarctica .Some goes to east others to west and some others to the south. The entire covered area was 1.5 million square miles (2.4 million Square km) in a total surface of 8.7 million square miles (14 million square km twice the surface of Australia).So the majority of the continent is not discovered until today even multiple next expeditions coming from different countries were not as big as the one of the USA and most of them were civilians not militaries.

The strange incident which was photographed by the US marine at that time in March 1947, declared by Admiral Byrd himself and it's leaked today was an attack from a group of flying saucers emerging from the ocean and open fire to the ships something was deeply shocking for the naval crew as it was the first time that they see something like that, especially the enormous speed of these UFOs and their capability to stop instantly taking other angles with 22 and 45 degrees.

Admiral Richard Byrd was obliged to deviates the direction of his Philippines Sea Ship to other one. Byrd declared: "A new enemy had been discovered it could fly from pole to pole in an instant".

Below sequences of the rare leaked footage recorded by US Soldiers in The Expedition .First of all a Nazi UFO pass through the middle of a ship from the right to the left of the camera. We see clearly the American Flag. The quality of the footage is ancient I tried to ameliorate the photos resolution the maximum possible:

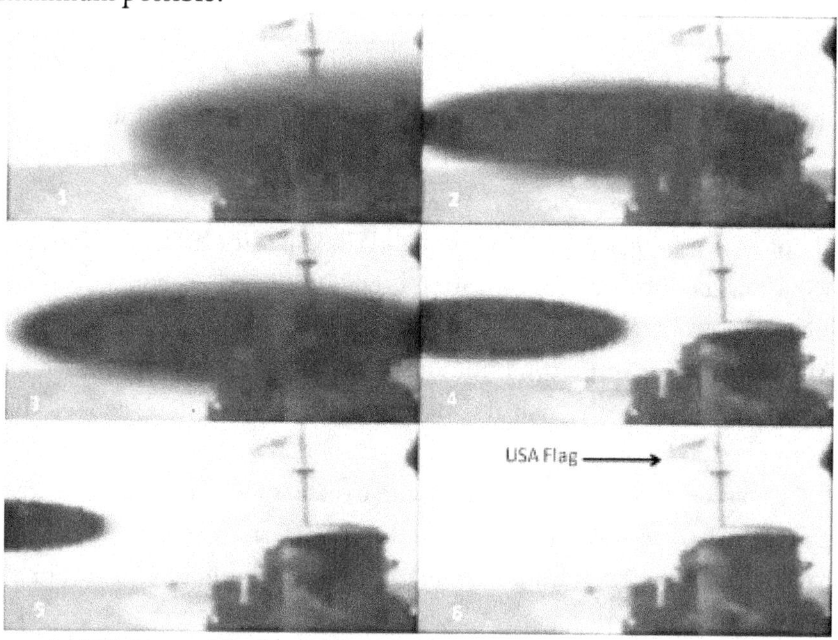

Nazi UFO Over a US Ship filmed by An American Soldier, The American Flag is very Clear

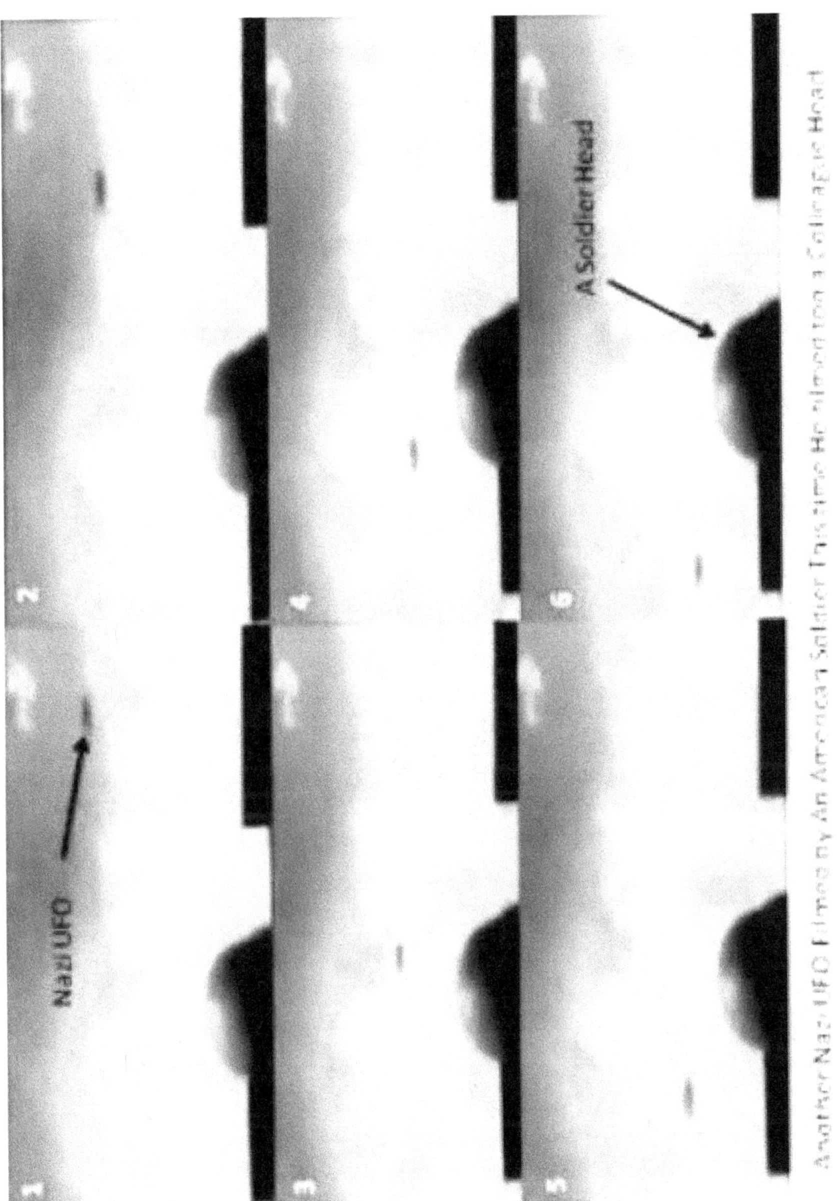

Another Nazi UFO filmed in another US Ship.The military helmet of a soldier appeared in the film:

The AirCrafts Carrier received Great Damage From The Nazis UFOs

AirCrafts Damaged Over The Ship

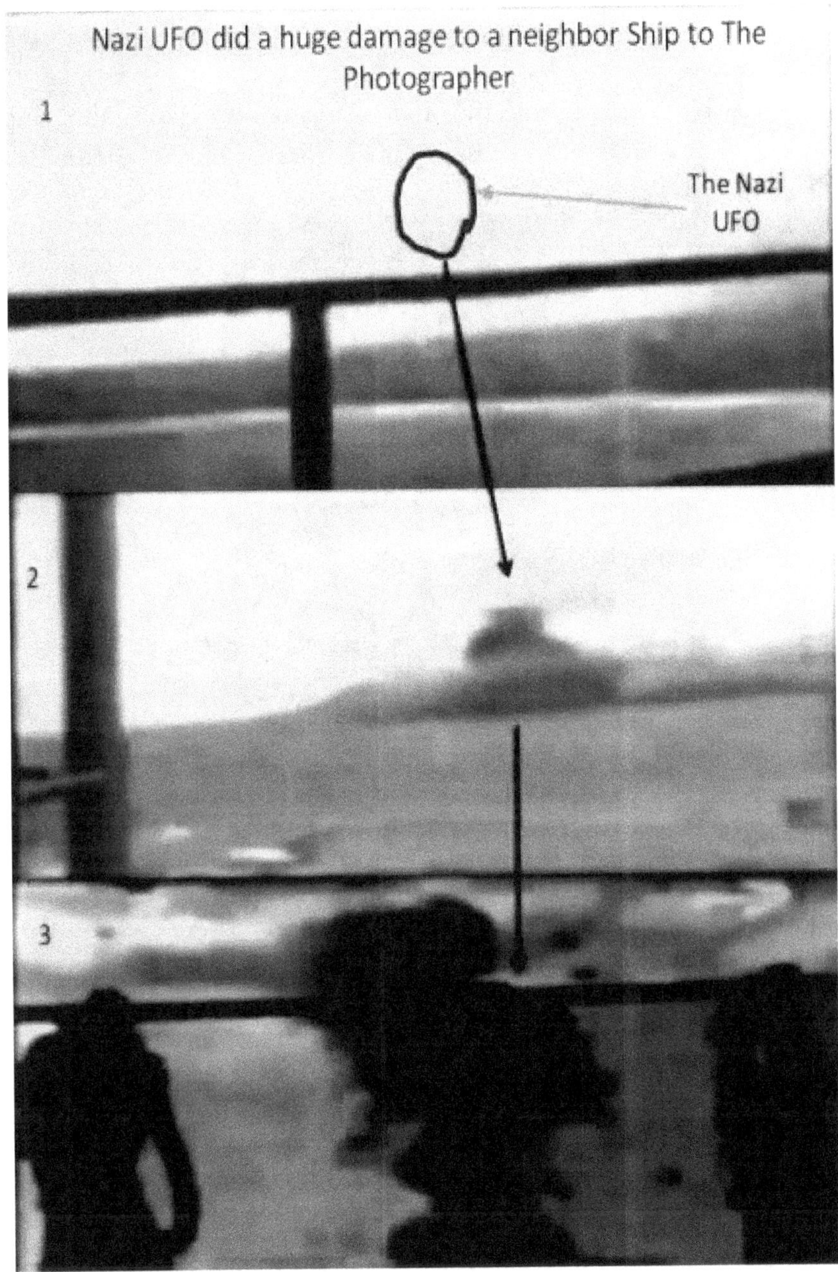
Nazi UFO did a huge damage to a neighbor Ship to The Photographer
1
The Nazi
UFO
2
3

Some planes were destroyed over the Aircrafts carrier, these images reflects this:

A Nazi UFO sent a projectile or an energy beam to a neighbor ship of the photographer and it made a huge damage that can't be done with normal or big bullets.

From a testimony of a soldier of the armada of Richard Byrd High Jump operation, he described the sink of a destroyer: "Suddenly Destroyer Murdock located ten cables from us has caught a bright flame of fire and begin sinking. All nightmare continued for about twenty minutes. When Flying Saucers dived again in the water, we started counting our losses, they were horrible"

The armada or small army sent to Antarctica was not for a simple expedition it was after the multiple sightings of UFOs with different shapes seen in the Atlantic and Pacific oceans and in the same time over the USA, Europe and Germany in the world war two. Those information were kept in secrecy until they sent this fleet to be reassured who are they exactly.

C.2: THE NAZIST SPACE PROGRAM

In the early March of 1937, a spherical flying saucer with a diameter of 11.5 feet (3.5 meters) landed in Munich Suburb in Southern Germany with three Aliens members who requested contact with the Country's Officials.

The image below show one of them between two volksturm or civilians police .They were named later "Areans" The documents and footages about these aliens and their flying saucers were either destroyed by allies bombs or taken by them as we can see his photos today.

The Nazis were aware of this incident and others , they put the flying machines under scientific and military research.

In this image two civilian police took the alien in a tour in the city's streets .Ordinary people could saw him without problem it was not a secret like it became later like in our days.

The spherical flying saucers or UFOs with this little diameter and little aliens on board were and are being seen worldwide especially in Mexico .They draw in the sky different forms aiming to send messages to humans.

At the end of World War II, the allies discovered secret Nazis experimental bases that revealed a highly sophisticated and technological development which largely exceeded the rest of the world. Some findings stills in secrecy and others are mediated , one of these discoveries, are sites of experiencing flying saucers named "ring test" or test rings(The Henge). those rings are connected to underground secret constructions :

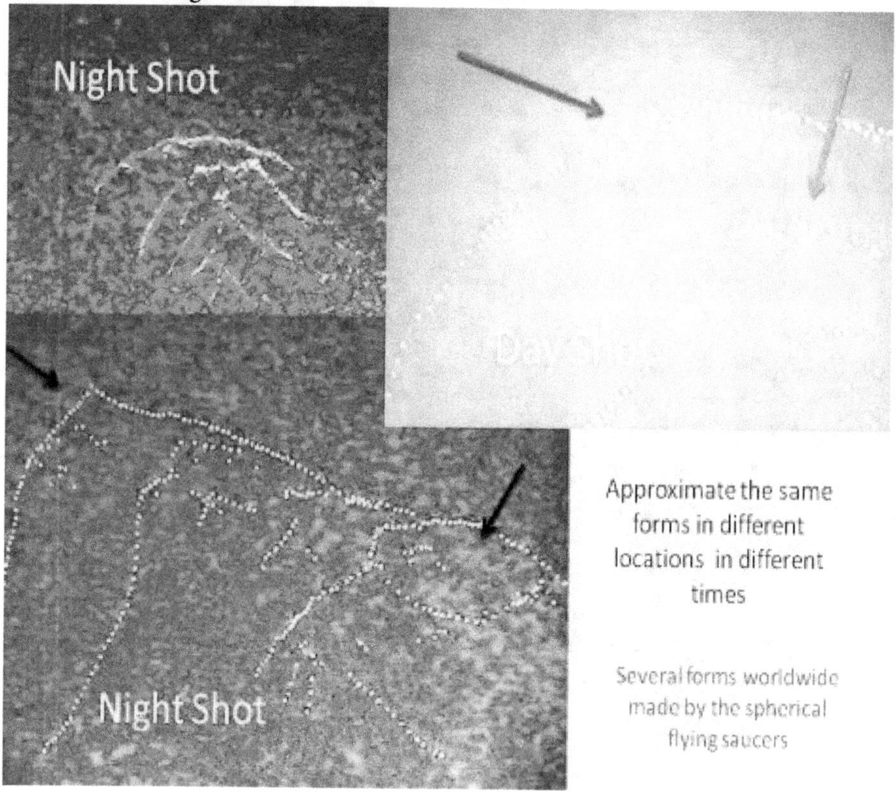

Approximate the same forms in different locations in different times

Several forms worldwide made by the spherical flying saucers

One Of Sites dedicated to test some Nazi's Flying Saucers

A story talks about a first sighting in Germany was in Munich in 1918 by a girl called Maria Orsic, who was contacted by aliens who come from star Aldebaran located in the constellation of Taurus 68 years in light from the earth but she couldn't translate what they said.

This girl transmitted the information to German officials who then investigated the case and be reassured about its credibility and with the help of another girl named Segrun, they could understood the speech of the visitors, they decided to give them somehow a Franchise by creating a secret society and program that will handle this case: VRIL, which is an abbreviation of the word: Verlieren and as their hairs were long hairs so they made it a slogan to this secret society.

German engineers have tried to duplicate the technology of these devices. When Adolf Hitler came to power he became interested about the subject .In 1945 the allies recovered Nazi technology and benefited from the enormous technological advances of German engineers in aviation: jet engines, rockets, mega machines, etc. Through the World War II the Nazis had families of jet engines.

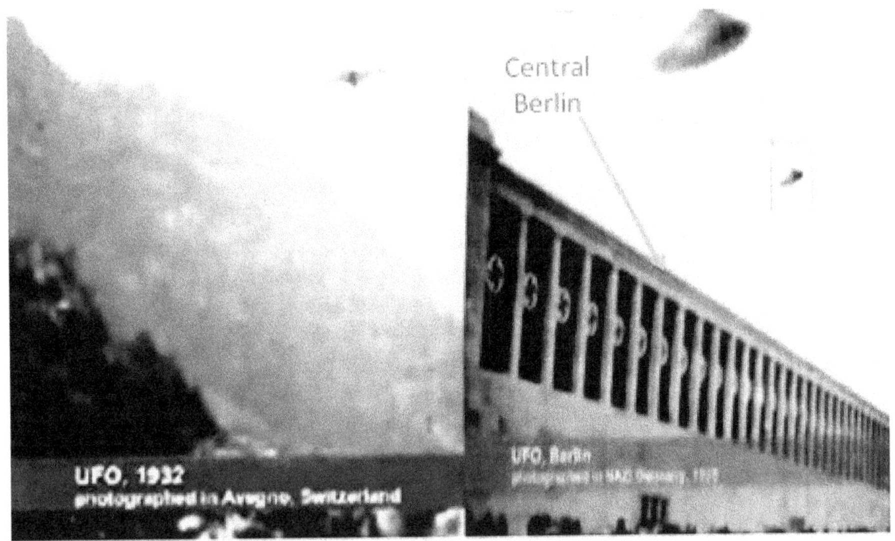

Two RFZ seen in Germany and Switzerland(next to Germany) in two different years 1932 and 1935

Americans have discovered several conceptions of space vessels. More than 1600 scientists and engineers have been transferred to the united states to work on special and secret projects as not to be judged as Nazis, one of them, the most influential was Werner von Braun, who was at the end of World War II, tried to hide prototypes, equipments and documents related to Nazis programs in a mountain cave, sixty-kilometers from Berlin.

The greatest discovery at that time, was the flying saucer experiments sites, something that has magnified the scenario of escape of Hitler, controversial to known history that he committed suicide with his mistress and their bodies were burned by their assistants and the Russians, but as it's known, no evidence of existence of their bodies.

The discovered designs has been used after the development of aeronautics in the united states and has sparked the interest of a U.S. program of space, Germany was more developed in this area, the U.S. has been concentrating on submarines and aircraft carriers.

During World War I, several pilots have seen unidentified flying objects in space of Germany .According to various sources, RFZ means RundFlugZeuge (round planes) or "Reichsflugzeuge", (the plane of the Reich).

This is the most mysterious series of UFO's Reich as so many prototypes has no pictures or plans. This probably comes from the fact that most documents on these devices have been destroyed or are still classified. Seven series of RFZ existed which the fifth and seventh series that took the name of a Haunebu I.

RFZ 1(1934):

The first German UFO was born in June 1934. It was led by Dr. Walter O. Schumann who was the first designer for the first circular experimental prototype of the aircraft factory Arado in Brandenburg : it was the RFZ 1. On his first flight was also the last, he rose vertically to a height of about 60 m and then began to twirl and dance in the air for several minutes.

The tail unit Arado 196 which was to guide the device proved completely inefficient. It is with great difficulty that the pilot Lothar Waiz succeeded to put it down, to escape and ran away from it because the machine began to spin like a top before it overturned and to be completely turn to pieces. It was the end of the RFZ 1, but the start of flying machines program VRIL.

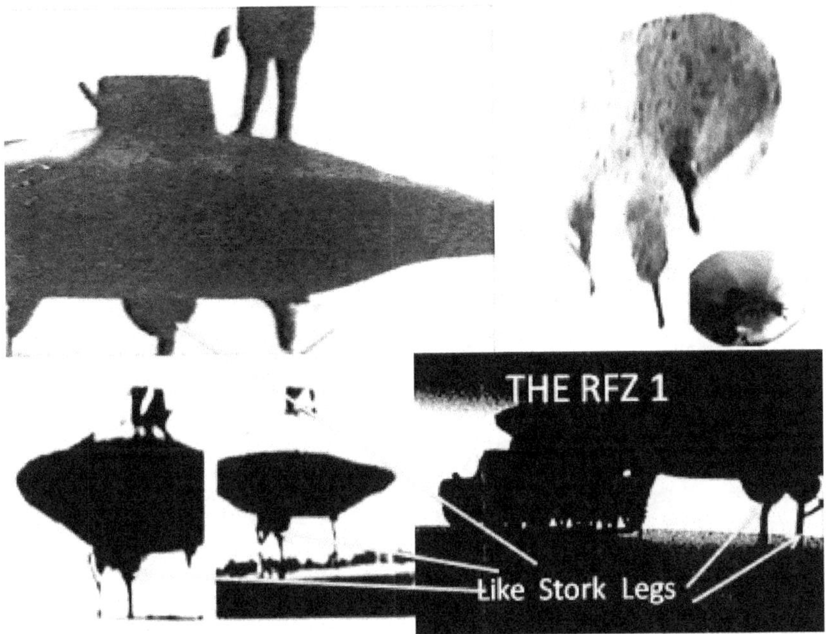

RFZ 2 (1934):

The RFZ 2 was finished before the end of 1934, he had Vril propulsion and a steering magnetic pulses .The contour of the unit faded when it's grows in speed and the machine lit up with different colors, which is a characteristic of UFOs. According to the propulsive force, it became red, orange, yellow, green, white, blue or purple. He could then run in 1941.

It was used as a reconnaissance aircraft over long distances during the Battle of Britain. Was photographed in late 1941 over the South Atlantic on his way to the auxiliary cruiser Atlantis in the waters of Antarctica. He could not be used as a fighter because of his driving pulse, the RFZ 2 could not make changes in direction of 90°, 45° or 22.5°.

It's amazing, some of these angle changes in flight that characterize the Nazi's UFOs and never the different fighters of today from different countries: USA, Russia, UK, France, Italy and China could do these angles even the 90° they never could do it properly. The Americans took an entire prototype.

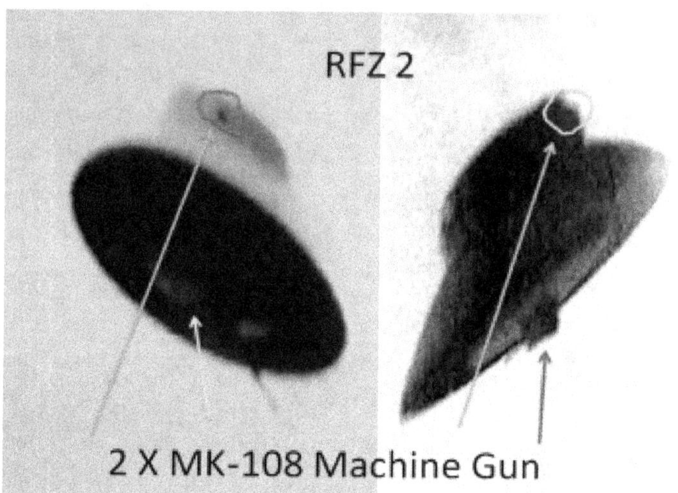
RFZ 2
2 X MK-108 Machine Gun

*Reichsflugzeuge 2 or Rund Flugzeuge 2 :
    *Diameter : 5m
    *Motor : Schuman-levitators
    *Driver : Mag-yeld-impulser 3a
    *Velocity: 6.000km/h (theorically up 24.000 km/h)
    *Armement : Mitrailleuse 2 x MK-108
    *Shielding : Unknown
    *Crow: 1 human.
    *Duration of stable fly: 12 minutes, day and night all times
    *First fly: 1934
    *date of running: 1941

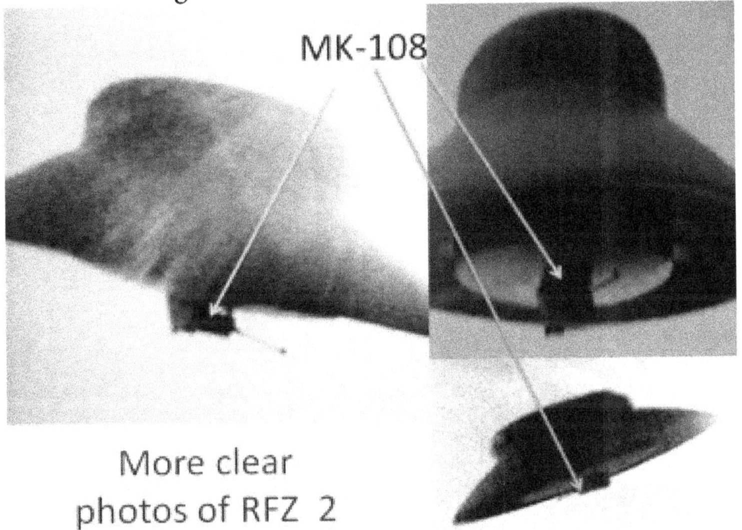

More clear
photos of RFZ 2

Another photo taken for the RFZ 2 under a Hydrogen balloon used widely in the first half of the twentieth century .The hydrogen is in abundance on water that's why the oil corporations Owners forbid it.

RFZ 2 Under A Nazi Hydrogen Balloon

RFZ 3(1936)

It was tested two different models of flying saucers FU 1 and FU2.

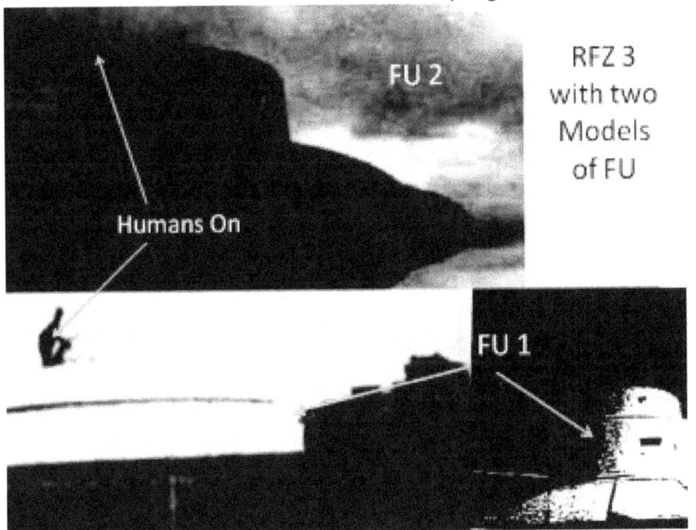

RFZ 4 (1935)

Even more mysterious than the RFZ 3, everything we know about him is that he was the forerunner of a Haunebu.

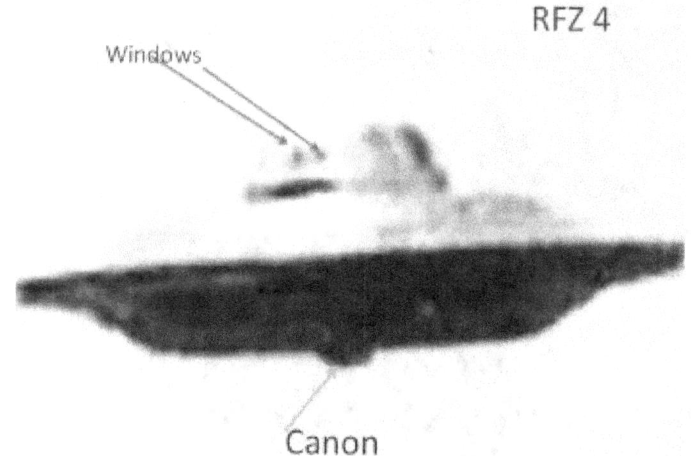

RFZ 5 (1939)
The RFZ 5 is an improvement of RFZ 4 and later became the Haunebu I.

RFZ 6 (1943)

It was a kind of supersonic aircraft. In 1941, Miethe and Shriver begun building the first V-7 makes its first fly near Prague in December 1942 under the name V-7 FlugKreisel.

With a height of 3m20 and 14m40 diameter, the device is powered by five tornado Shauberger reactors, two of them take the horizontal translation and the other three involve a variable pitch rotor for vertical take-off and sustenance:

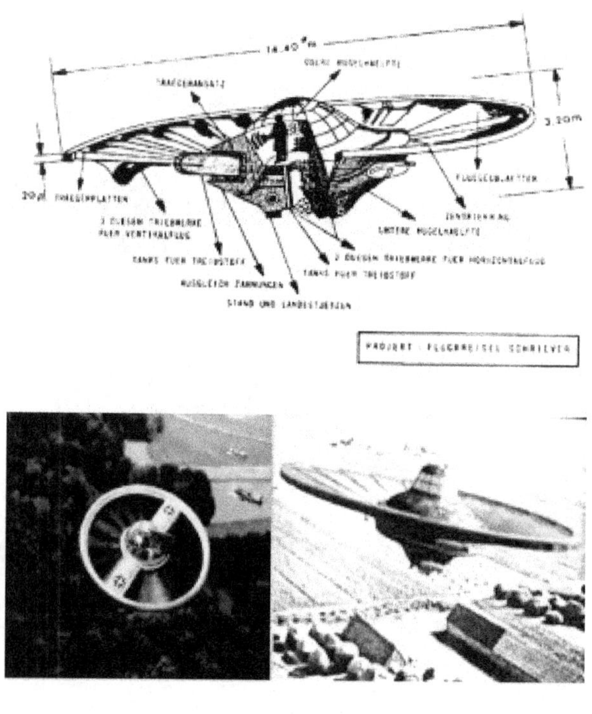

RFZ 6

*Reichsflugzeuge 6 or Rund Flugzeuge 6

*Diameter : 14.40m

*Motor : Unknown

*Driver : Unknown

*Velocity : 100km/h

*Armament : Unknown

*Shielding : Unknown

*Crow : 1 human

*Duration of stable fly: 5 to 10 min

*First fly : 1943

*Date of running : 1944

RFZ 7 (1945)

The RFZ 7 is a Coanda saucer it uses a different method of propulsion than RFZ 6. It would be a sort of UFO for troop transport .It's took so attention the sophistication of German technology at the end of World War II and the extraordinary range of weapons known as "Vengeance" with Hitler hoped at the last moment, turn the phase of the war with a final surprise.

Only two of them, the V-1 and V-2 ballistic missile, were officially used. But at the end of the war and during the cold war in the western Germany exploring the documentation and the secret laboratories carefully camouflaged, the Allies realized the degree of completion of the research by scientists to serve the Hitler cause: they found scattered traces including an array of secret programs like Haunebu, Vril and others.

It has been claimed that these acquisitions from the third Reich, can help the Allies in technology for developing their own flying saucers, but somehow evidences are lacking: the Germans have destroyed a large number of secret bases at the time of the falling. But this couldn't forbid the allies to own their own technology on this field later.

Rudolph Schriever

In spring 1941, Rudolph Schriever, an aeronautical engineer of the Luftwaffe, called the father of Nazi RFZ and the designer of Haunebu program has received the help of two German engineers : Miethe and Habermohl and the support of an Italian named Giuseppe Belluzzo to complete the unit. This poses some interrogations about the real origin of the RFZ program.

Draws supposed to Belluzzo:

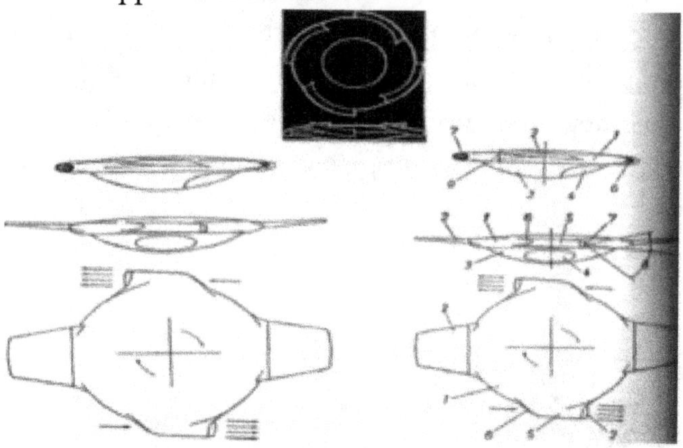

Draws of UFOs Discs supposed to be for Giuseppe
Belluzzo

The documents that would resolve this conflict of real origin , it's assumed generally that the engineers who were engaged in the development of flying discs for the Nazis, originally they designed those engines to be powered with turbine gases, then they modified this budget with an advanced form of propulsion reaction.

So, Rudolph Schriever, Walter Miethe and Klaus Habermohl were the first conceivers of the project of a Haunebu 1, a reaction disk with a ring pivoting around a fixed cabin-shaped dome. The disc was wing-shaped mobile adjustable depending on the take-off or the flying height.

Another earthy flying saucer device, with vectorial propulsion, designed by Professor Miethe, was 42 meters in diameter. After being tested in Prague, February 14th , 1945, this unit took the name of V-8.

This device can amounting to over ten kilometers in less than three minutes, reaching speeds of 2000 km / h in horizontal flight performance far sophisticated than others at that time.

Photos of flying saucer February 14th, 1945 In Prague Sky

Other drawings of Miethe discs, assumed to be the first to have leaked, devoided of technical details, do provide the interiors above and below the fuselage of the disk, with two engines was in the back reaction, the whole resembling a strangely B2 stealth aircraft .

Other Miethe draws:

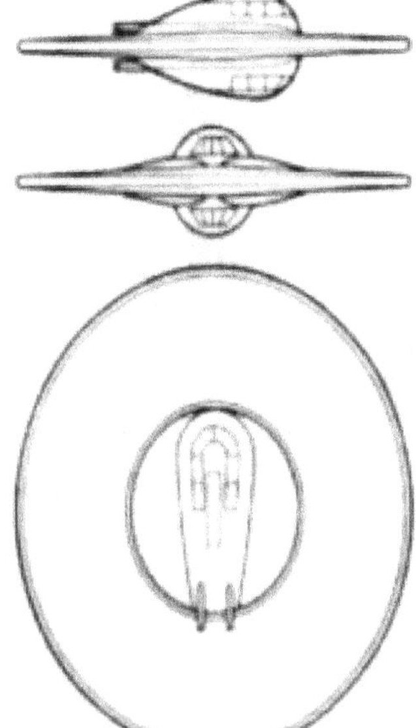

Other Miethe Discs
Plans and Prototypes

The government of West Germany has Schriever plans disc that would draws for Hitler, but in aeronautics, specialists say they have been falsified and rendered unusable. Anyway, the simple drawing showing a record of 15 meters in diameter four feet is conceptually very ahead of its time. It would have been equipped with futuristic technology, including a laser system, a radar and electromagnetic turbines.

According to American ufologist, retired Colonel Stevens Wendelle, These were a combination knowledge to new energy technologies developed by engineers from the work of the Austrian Viktor Schauberger, inventor of machines operated by "spirals inwards , "in which the energy was the result of implosions rather than explosions of internal combustion engine.

Viktor Schauberger showed holding his implosion device, which is claimed to be the basis for Nazi Antigravity research

Viktor Schauberger showed holding his implosion device, which is claimed to be the basis for Nazi Antigravity research.

Schauberger was very implicated in the design of human or terrestrial flying saucers that had been seen during World War II in four corners of the earth, he concepted several flying discs with a mode of "liquid vortex propulsion", a technology that would nullify earth gravity.

The Vril Society had experimented several singular technologies, including the Hans Kohler converter and "tachyon with Kohler magneto-gravitational transmission ", better known under the name "Thule tachyonateur " Vril discs with 10 meters diameters, highly sophisticated, were designed for aircraft interception battles. Propulsion technology with electromagnetic field would have been used in 1943 to destroy the Allied bombers that attacked ball bearings factories in Schweinfurt.

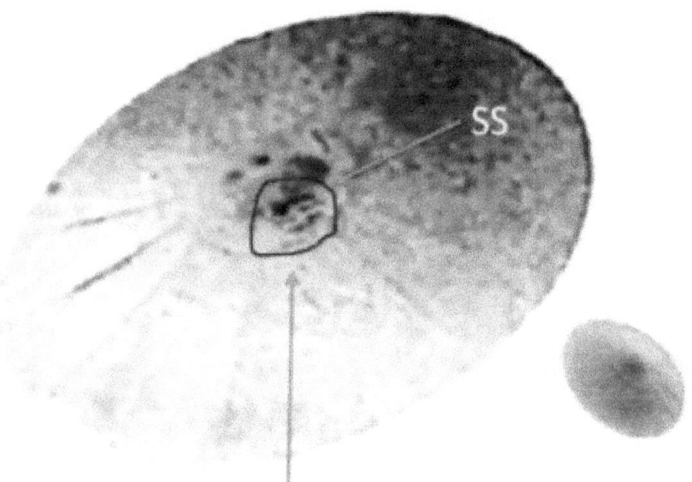

The Metallic Stamp Of SS(SchutzStaffel) Logo Is Clear On A One Of Nazis UFOs proving Their Real Existence.

The evidence of the existence of Vril or Haunebu equipments presented in the documents of SS:***Schutzstaffel(protection body)*** or ⚡⚡[1] founded in April 1925, and so many photos published, beside the prototypes taken by the united states after the WWII in secrecy with 1600 German scientists, in "Paperclip Operation" , that had the great cause for the development of The United States.

---

1.   http://en.wikipedia.org/wiki/File:Schutzstaffel_SS_SVG1.1.svg

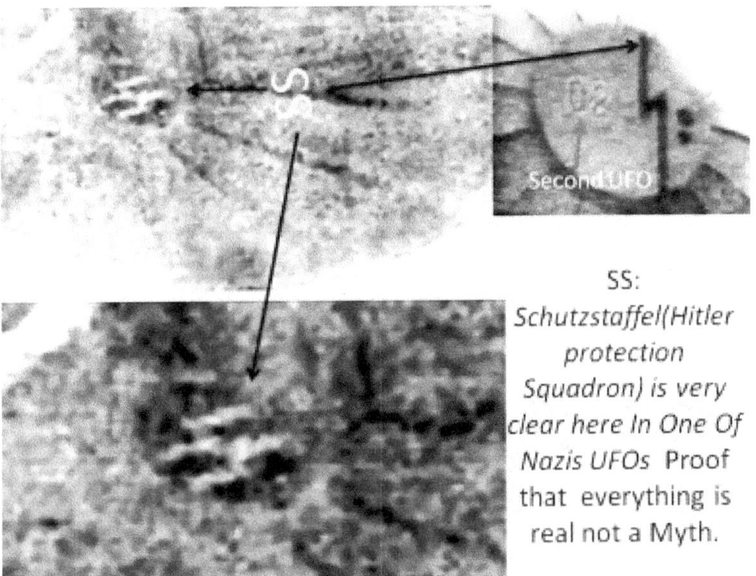

SS:
*Schutzstaffel(Hitler
protection
Squadron) is very
clear here In One Of
Nazis UFOs* Proof
that everything is
real not a Myth.

But so many historians, have a doubt for the real existence in the war and were not just a papers conceptions because those devices have not succeeded in controversy the balance in favor of the Nazis. In deed some devices did exist but they were discreetly camouflaged in mountains caves in Germany and precisely in Berlin and Munich and some others were out of Germany waiting just before the defeat for better days.

In 1938, Hitler sent so many expeditions to the Antarctica traced the map of a region of Queen Maud Land that the Nazis renamed Neu Schwabenland :

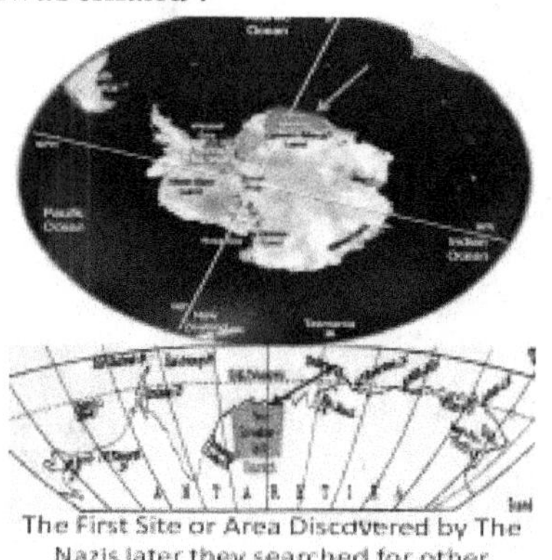

The First Site or Area Discovered by The Nazis later they searched for other places

Photos from expedition in Antarctica:

Nazis Soldiers With The Nazi Flag In Antarctica

This very wide area included several areas with no ice. Throughout the war, the Nazis have bring so different materials to build huge secret bases.

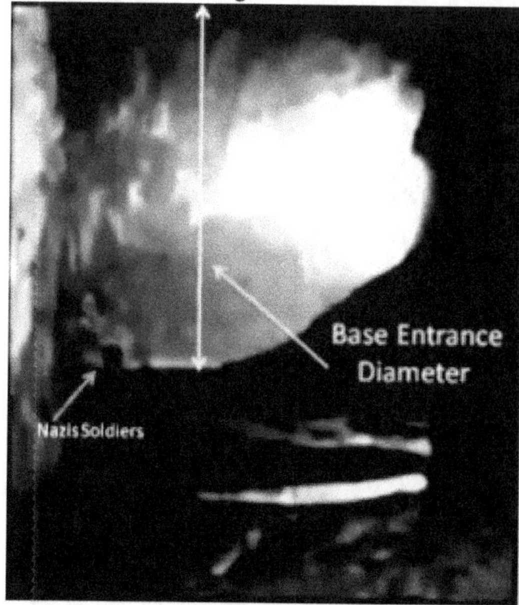

Huge Base or Cave Entrance In comparison with The Nazis Soldiers Size. Huge Nazis UFOs can enter through it.

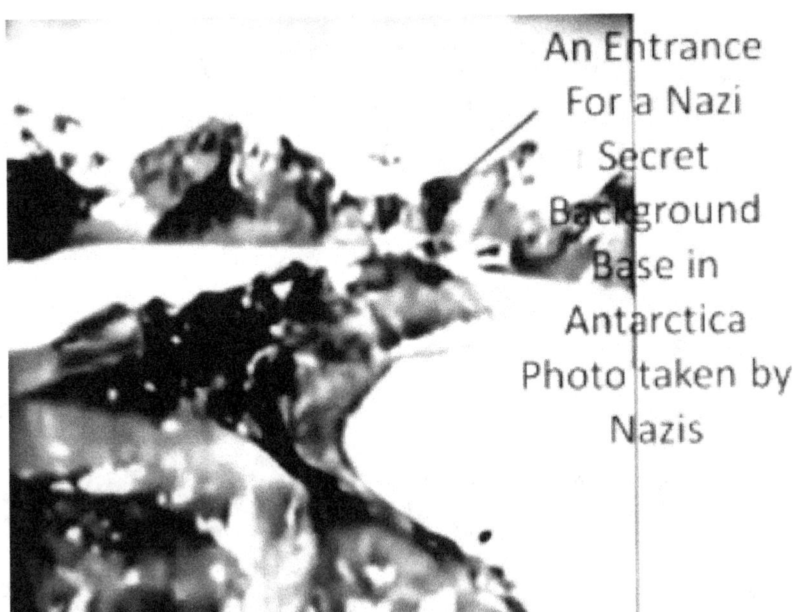
An Entrance
For a Nazi
Secret
Background
Base in
Antarctica
Photo taken by
Nazis

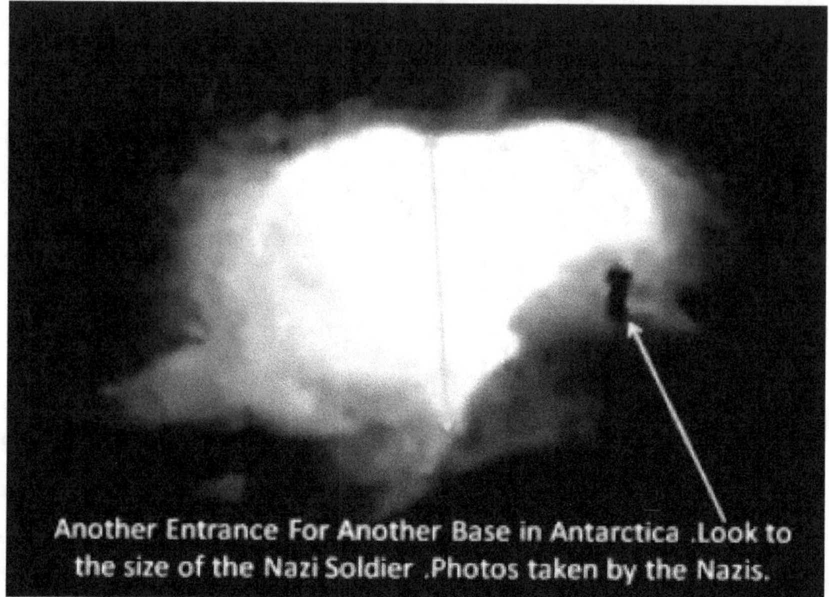

Another Entrance For Another Base in Antarctica .Look to
the size of the Nazi Soldier .Photos taken by the Nazis.

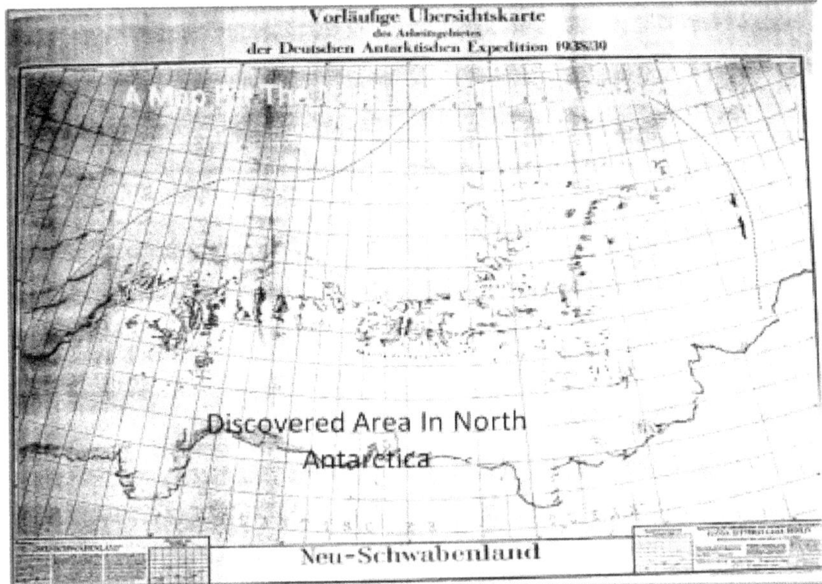
Vorläufige Übersichtskarte
des Arbeitsgebietes
der Deutschen Antarktischen Expedition 1938/39
Discovered Area In North
Antarctica
Neu-Schwabenland

Original Nazi Map For their Colonies in Northern Antarctica

In these bases the Nazis had constructed submarines and so many flying saucers projects .In the late fifteenth, in 1947 the Americans tried to discover the base and to take it with force from the Nazis with an operation called:" High Jump", but they couldn't because the Germans were more developed, beside this the Americans wanted that all the operations still in secrecy without the press knowledge.

In 2011, the United States ordered all the scientific expeditions from all the world to leave the Antarctica and that's made Europe sending a blame to the U.S and demanded an explanation to this abnormal, not request but an order.

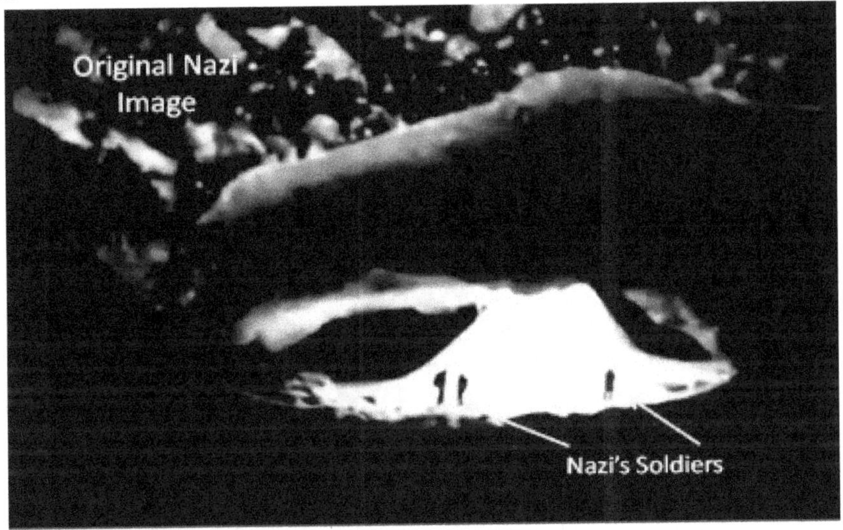

Huge Underground Cave in Antarctica.

The international mainstream press and media didn't talk seriously about this subject and it was intentional .The Americans wanted to surrounding the story and make it under control but leaked photos showed the real cause behind this order which is the discovery of a flying saucer by a scientific expedition.

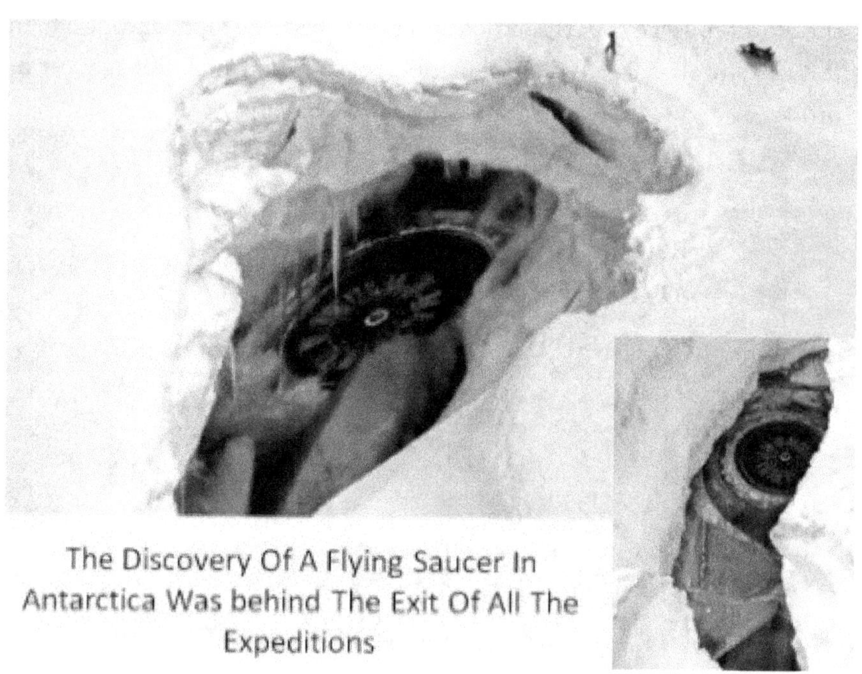

The Discovery Of A Flying Saucer In Antarctica Was behind The Exit Of All The Expeditions

what we see today
amateurs videos UFO
ing in Volcanos eruption
mouths and in moutains
Nazi UFO Over
Antarctica.Photo
taken by Nazis

Dr Walter Miethe, as many German scientists, would have been recruited by the Americans and Canadians to resume his previous work for Germany in the U.S, like Werner von Braun, the designer of the V-2, who has been working on the American space programs." Other American secret documents service from 1955 provided the construction by the Canadian company A. V. Roe, a reaction disc capable of reaching Mach 3.4 (3.4 times the speed of sound).

The Haunebu series was treated by Professor Walter O. Schumann, in friendly competition with Victor Schauberger who was the manager of Vril series, moreover, he gave the Vril 5 motors to equip Haunebu I. The autonomy of Haunebu was higher than Vril. Indeed, if one compares the Vril to hunters, Haunebu would be bombers.

The Haunebu II is the most famous of the Nazi saucers as she was often photographed in the world in the '50s, including George Adamski ones. The Americans have even recovered a complete copy. As for the Haunebu III, investigators has doubts remains about its implementation. The Haunebu IV some think it remains in the phase of plan and the least known of the series.

Circular windows as seen in Haunebu Models :

Internal View Of One Of Haunebu Models

HAUNEBU I (1939)

The Haunebu I is the fifth version of the mysterious series RFZ. Although we have photographs and plans, but it still considered the most unknown saucer of the series after the Haunebu IV.

Equipped with motors that Schauberger kindly gave to Schuman, she is unstable in flight and can fly perfectly for 8 minutes. The machine gun turret, made the dish unstable. Subsequently, the Nazis were planning to use a kind of laser called the "death ray" instead of the machine gun.

Original Datasheet For The Haunibu I Model

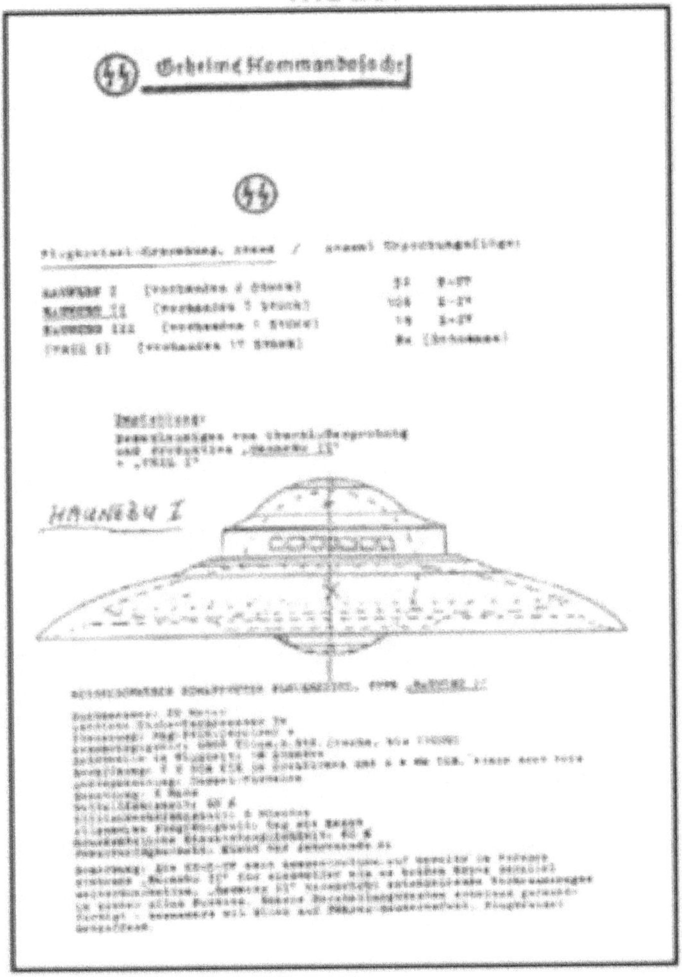

This original document signed from the SS and presents a datasheet or technical details for the Haunebu I composed from a technical draw, information about the infrastructure of the Haunebu I .This document give also, some information about the available flying saucers constructed from the third Reich. We can conclude easy that the most available machine is VRIL I with a 17 articles.

The less number in all the machines is the Haunebu III, just one article .Then we found the Haunebu I with 2 and the Haunebu II with 7 articles .We found also the number of flight made by every model, the Haunebu I , 52 times, Haunebu II,106 times, Haunebu III,19 times and the Vril I ,84 times.

*Gyroscopic Kompass moderately armed.

*Diameter : 25 m

*Motor : Thule Tachyonator (Triebwerk) 7b

*Driver : Field Impulser 4

*Velocity : 4.800km/h (theorically can rise 17.000km/h)

*Armament : Canons 2 x 80 mm KSK on rotating turret ; canons 4 x MK-108

*Shielding : Double Victalen

*Crow : 8 humans

*Duration of stable fly : 8 minutes, day and night for all times.

*First fly : 1939

*Date of running or working: 1944

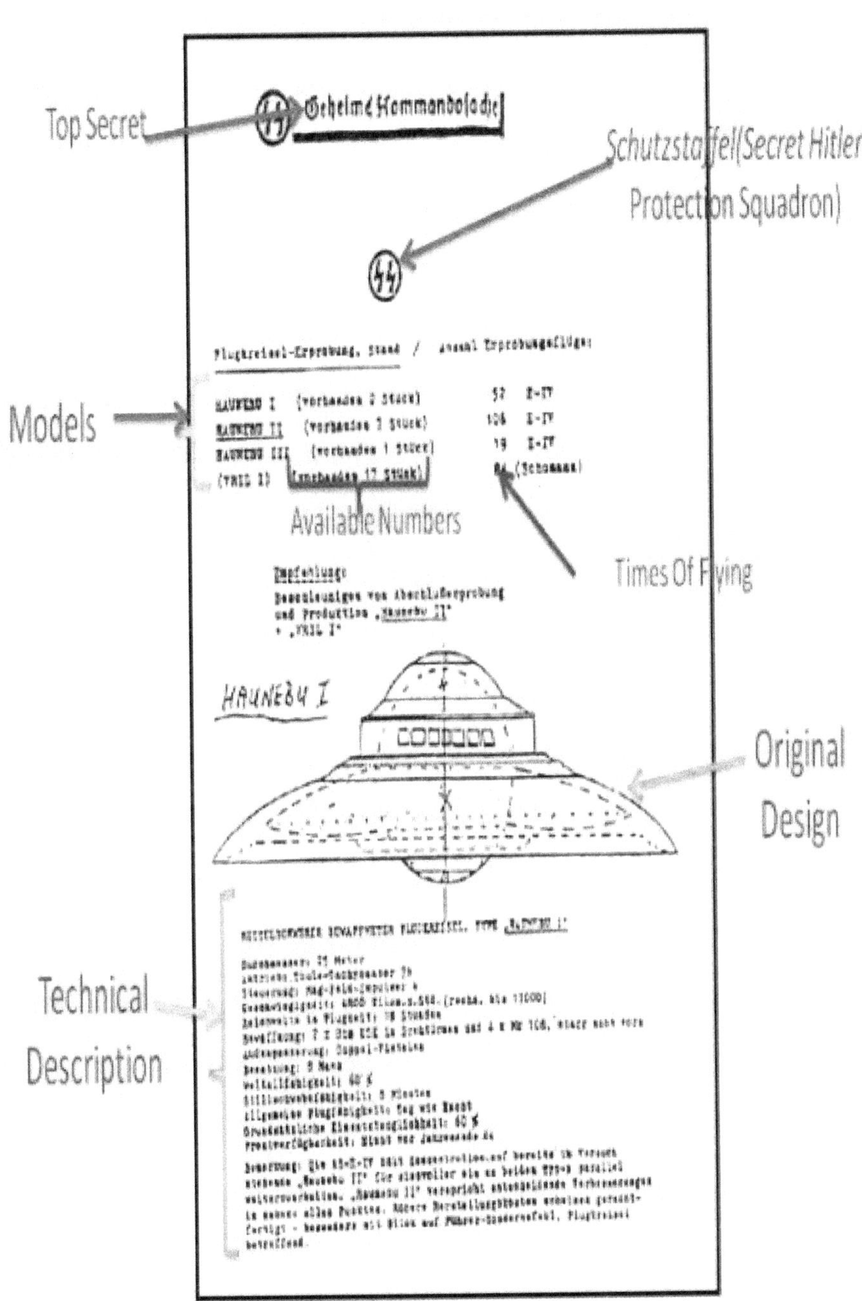
Top Secret
Schutzstaffel(Secret Hitler Protection Squadron)
Models
Available Numbers
Times Of Flying
Original Design
Technical Description
HAUNEBU I

HAUNEBU II (1940)

The Haunebu II is the most famous machine of this series because it was often seen and photographed after the war world II. During these sightings, some people believed wrongly that its diameter was only 10 meters. More importantly, it is one of little machines that Americans have recovered complete. This is also the latest known version of the built Haunebu series and some sources assert that she was the example model for all American saucers built after the war.

This is also an original document from the third Reich dated from November 7th 1943.It's contains a technical draw with four huge balls, three of them, everyone has two machines guns, so it's composed from six machines gun The most huge ball is in the center of the Haunebu II .We can see also some circular windows with a number of six also in one side so twelve in all the circular form .This is the original Datasheet of Haunebu II:

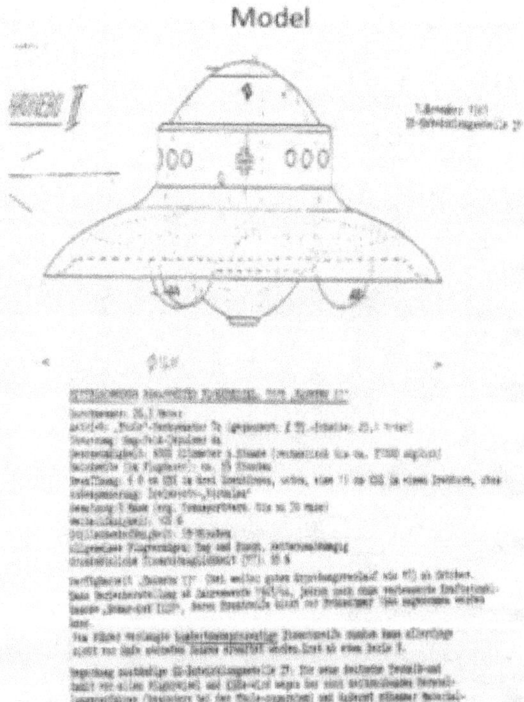

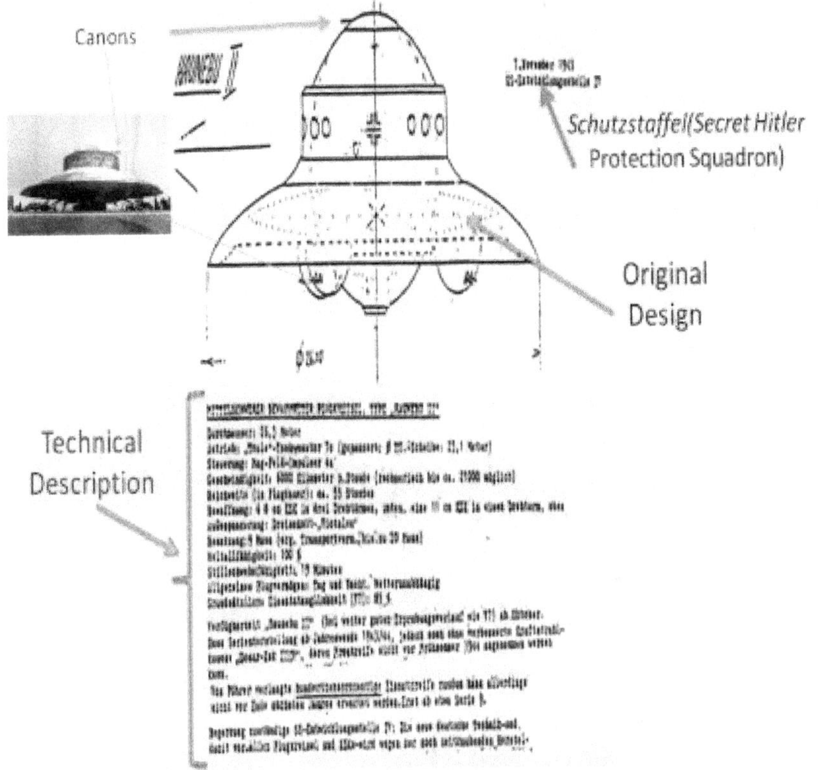
Canons
Schutzstaffel(Secret Hitler Protection Squadron)
Original Design
Technical Description

This is an original photo from the secret archive of the SS and Third Reich .The photos shows a machine of Haunebu II in a secret base in front of it discussing some army commanders and generals.

This photo shows also another machine gun in the up of Haunebu II and a number of 15, but as the information provided in the original document of the Haunebu I, the Haunebu II available number at that time was 7 articles.

Haunibu II Standing In One Of Nazis Bases

What we can conclude from this photo two possibilities: the first one that the Haunebu II produced more than 7 and this is very possible because it's the most famous and successful model; the second possibility that this photo is for a developed and ameliorated model for Vril I as we know it was produced with 17 articles available and Schauberger gave the motor of Vril to Schauman with Haunebu.

*Gyroscopic Kompass highly armed

*Diameter : 26.30m

*Motor : Thule Tachyonator (Triebwerk)·7c

*Driver : Field Impulser 4a

*Velocity : 6.000km/h (theorically up 21.000km/h)

*Armament : canons 6 x 80mm KSK on 3 rotating turrets; canon 1 x 110mm KSK rotating turrets.

*Shielding : Victalen triple

*Crew: 9 humans (can bring 20 persons for the transport)

*Duration of stable fly : 8 minutes, day and night all the times.

Duration of a complete Fly : 55 heures

*First Fly : 1942

*Date of running or working : 1944.

The Haunebu II is approximately the same design as the design of the Venusian who met George Adamski or from the Moon bases That's gives a scenario that the Venusians or Mooners are maybe the sons of Hitler: The Aryans, who weren't know their fathers and mothers and can't speak English language, he sent them to Venus and/or Moon. Without exaggeration this can be .The same for the case of Elizabeth Klarer in UK with Akon he too mostly from The Aryans.

One Of Haunebu II Models Do-Stra :

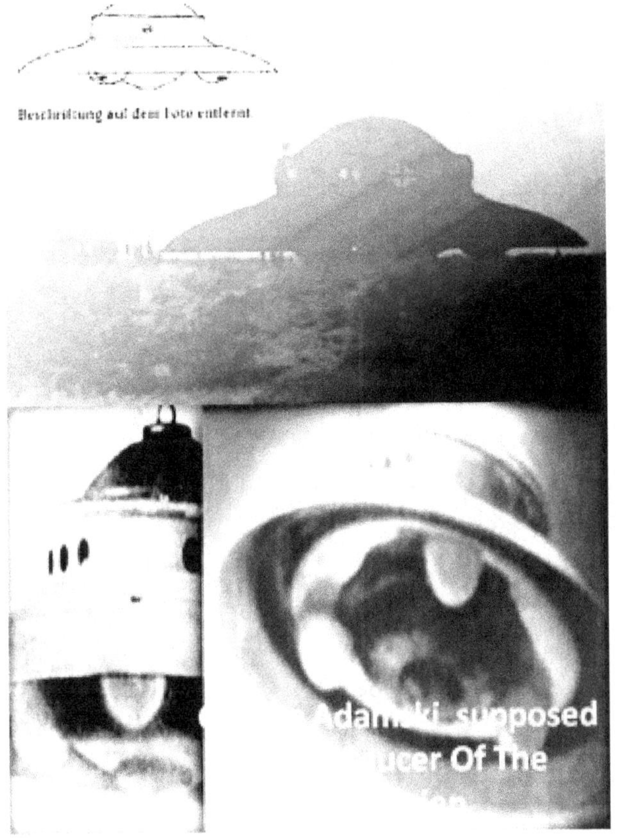
Beschriftung auf dem Foto entfernt.
Adamski supposed
ucer Of The

HAUNEBU III (1944)

The Haunebu III was a gigantic version of Haunebu series. It uses an antigravity propulsion system like the others. Its dimensions were absolutely gigantic with 71 meter in diameter! Its armament was also impressive, combining simple electromagnetic machine guns and canons! Its autonomy was also astonishing , it can fly 7 to 8 weeks without stopping it's like what we see in the so called "science fiction" movies and cartoons.

*Heavily Armed Flight Gyro

*Diameter: 71 m

*Drive: Thule Tachyonator (Thule Triebwerk) 7c plus SM-Levitators

*Driver: Mag Field Impulser 4a

*Velocity : 7,000 km/h (theoretically up to 40,000 km/h)

*Range: Flight time 7 to 8 weeks

*Armament: 4 x 110 mm KSK in 4 rotating turrets (3 lower/1 upper)/10 x 80 mm KSK in rotating turrets plus 6 x MK 108/8 x 50 mm KSK

*Shielding: Triple Victalen

*Crew: 32 (with room for up to 70 people)

*Quiet flight: 25 minutes

All weather, day and night, capability

*Employment fitness: 100%

*First flight: 1945

*Available for service: 1945

Original Datasheet for the Haunebu III Model:

Original Datasheet Of Haunibu III

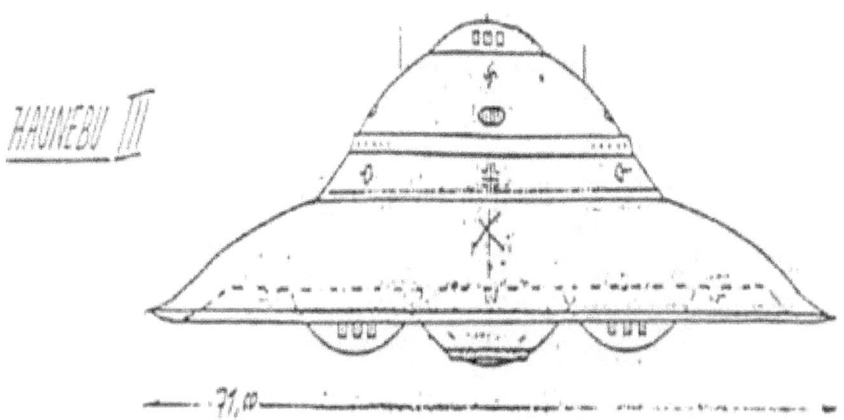

SCHWERER BEWAFFNETER FLUGKREISEL "HAUNEBU III"

Durchmesser: 71 Meter
Antrieb: Thule-Tachionator 7b plus Schumann-Levitatoren (gepanzert)
Steuerung: Mag-Feld-Impulser 4a.
Geschwindigkeit: ca. 7000 Kilom.p.Stunde (rechnerisch bis zu 40000)
Reichweite (in Flugdauer): ca. 8 Wochen (bei S-L-Flug 40% mehr)
Bewaffnung: 4 x 11cm KSK in Drehtürmen (3 unten, 1 oben), 10 x 8cm KSK
in Drehringen plus 6 x MK 108, 8 x 8cm KSK ferngesteuert
Außenpanzerung: Dreinschott-Victalen
Besatzung: 32 Mann (erg. Transportverm. max. 70 Personen)
Weltallfähigkeit: 100 %.
Stillschwebefähigkeit: 25 Minuten.
Allgemeines Flugvermögen: Wetterunabhängig Tag und Nacht
Grundsätzliche Einsatztauglichkeit: Etwa 1945.

Bemerkung: SS-E-IV hält den Hinweis für notwendig, daß in
"Haunebu III" ein großartiges Werk deutscher Technik im ent-
stehen ist, wegen der allgemeinen Materiallage aber alle
Kräfte auf das schneller verfügbare Haunebu II gesetzt
werden sollten.
Gemeinsam mit dem leichten Flugkreisel "Vril" der Schumann-
Gruppe könnte "Haunebu II" die vom Führer aufgestellten
Forderungen sicherlich erfüllen.

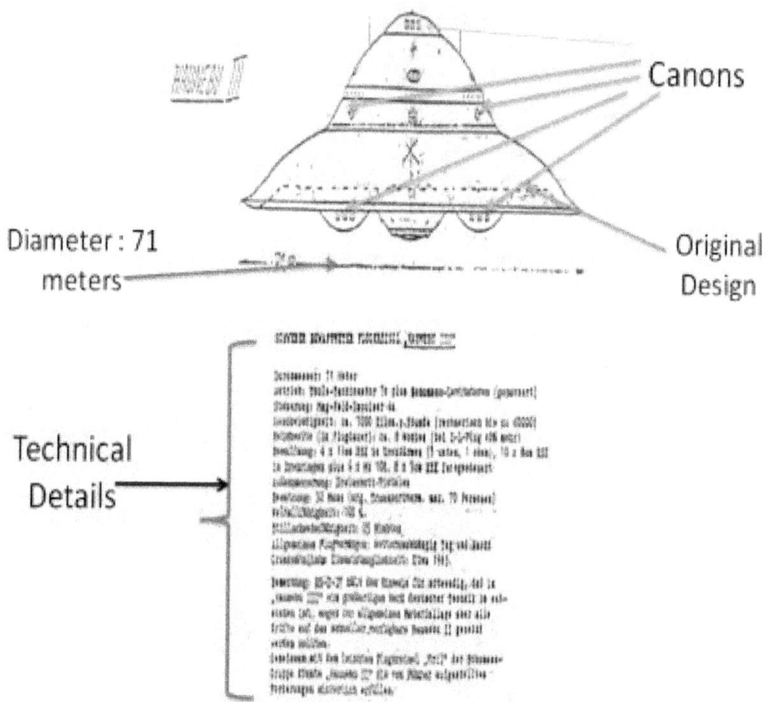

Diameter : 71 meters
Canons
Original Design
Technical Details

Haunebu III In Action . The Same as
the Original Datasheet

HAUNEBU IV (1945)

Much larger than the Haunebu III, it was supposed to be reserved for transporting troops and equipments.

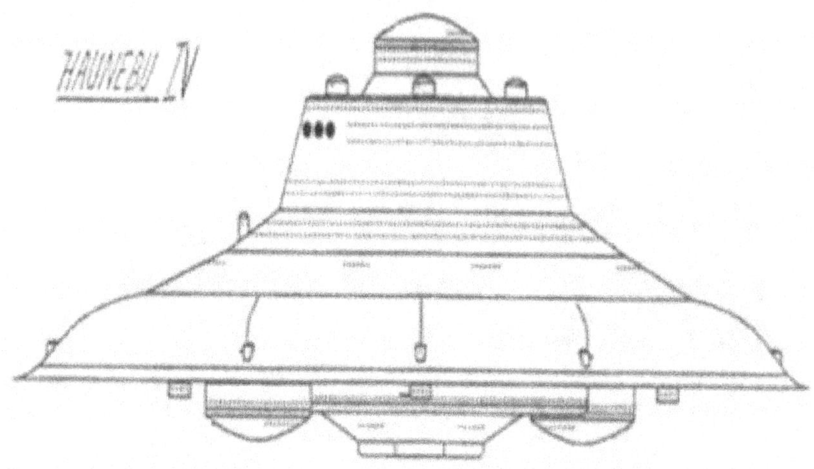

Haunebu IV with a diameter of 120 meters designed for troops transportation.

*Heavily Armed Flight Gyro

*Diameter : 120 meters.

*Seen in and after 1946 despite the end of the world war II.

VRIL SERIES :

The series of Vril is the best known achievements of Victor Schauberger. The first prototypes are the first military use of flying saucers. From Vril 1 until Vril 4, were very powerful engines but everything changes with the implementation of the Vril 5: great competitor to Shauberger Haunebu who generously gave his motor.

The double and triple shielding "victalen" is a special alloy, the famous "Impervium" material that offers high conductivity and a large friction resistance. For the autonomy of the vessels, it was theoretically unlimited, just for the subject to regular replacement of spare parts.

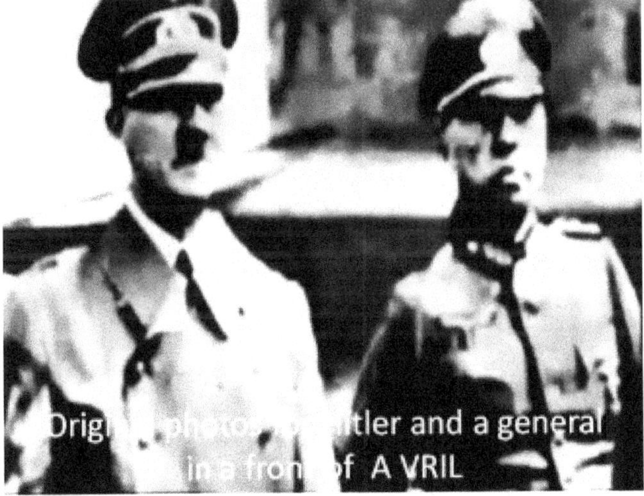

VRIL I (1934)

The Vril 1, the first series of "Vril", built from year 1934 to 1942, remained at the prototype stage, but it flew! It was equipped with a cockpit in plexiglass on the top. The designer was Schauberger and his team. This vessel would be loaded on other project named Andromeda with two others Vril 1 and a Haunebu I or II.

Original Photos of VRIL I:

Laser Gun
Original
Photos of VRIL
I Nazi's UFO
with some
construction
Stages

This draw below, shows the original Datasheet of two versions of Vril I .The first version is for the Vril I with a Laser Gun, the cockpit is with plexiglass like the Vril I model in the images up and not like the datasheet design. In this case its technical specifications are not completely like in the datasheet .The second version is like the technical specifications description especially the armament part, this version is the Jager Hunter version.

Original Datasheet For Vril I

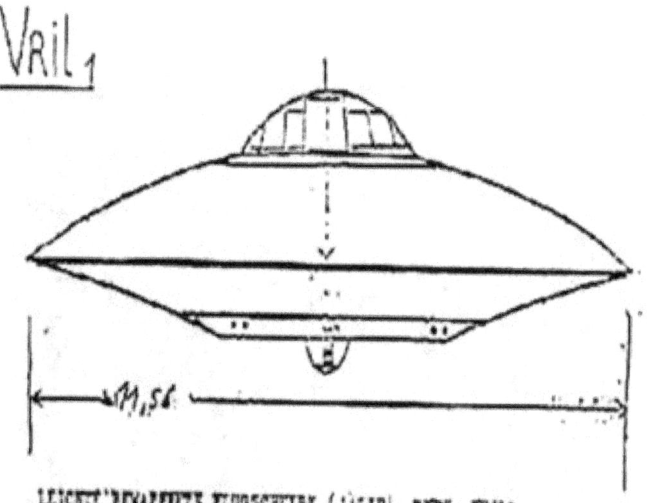

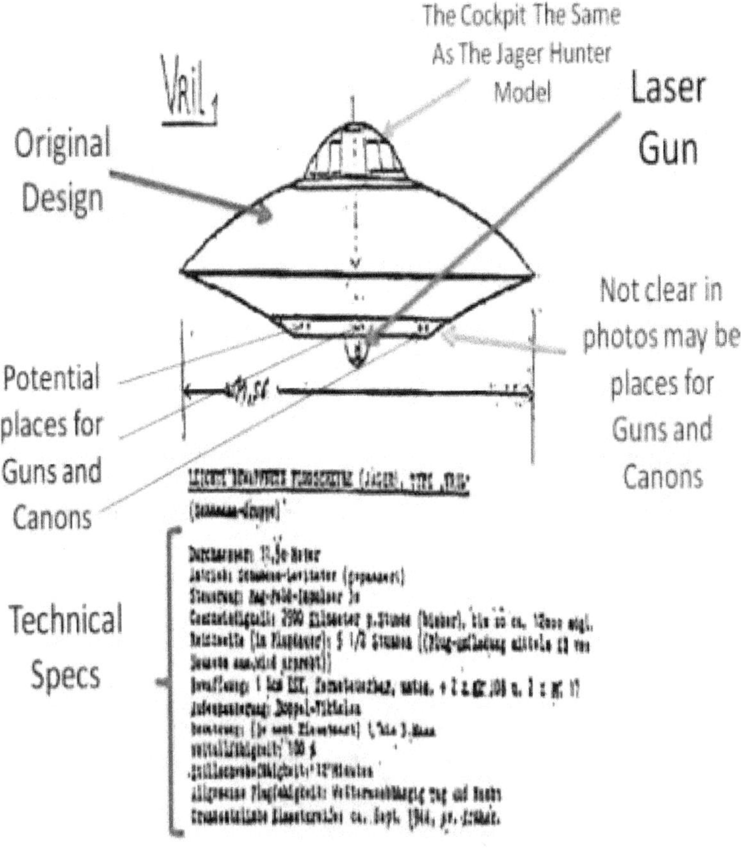
Vril₁
The Cockpit The Same
As The Jager Hunter
Model
Laser
Gun
Original
Design
Not clear in
photos may be
places for
Guns and
Canons
Potential
places for
Guns and
Canons
Technical
Specs

*Leich bewapphete flugscheibe (Jager Hunter) Vril 1(1934)

*Diamètre : 11.50m

*Motor : Schuman-levitators

*Driver : Mag-yeld-impulser 3a

*Velocity : 2.900 km/h (theoretically up 12.000km/h)

*Armament: Canons 1 x 80mm KSK on rotating turrets; machine guns: 2 x MK-108(Laser Gun For No Jager Hunter).

*Shielding: Double Victalen

*Crew : 1 human.

*Duration of stable fly: 12 minutes day and night with all weather conditions.

*First Fly: 1939

*Date of running or working: 1944 constructed in 18 prototypes.

Jager Hunter(VRIL)

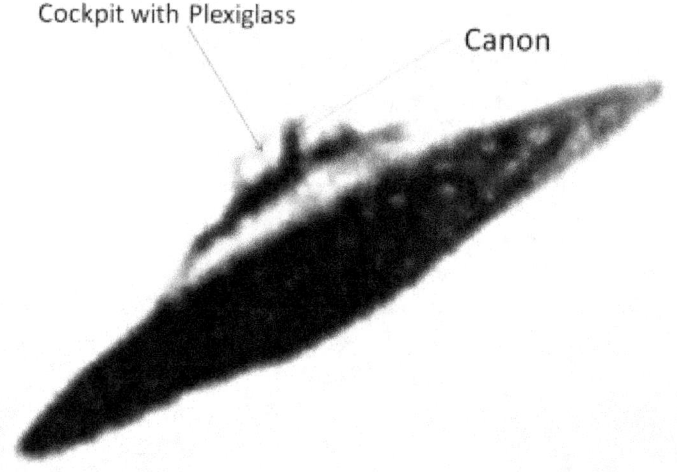

Jager Hunter a VRIL series Version

VRIL II(1936)

The Vril 2 is a more powerful version of the Vril 1. The cockpit Plexiglas Vril 1 was replaced by a pressurized cockpit topped with a metal bulb and Plexiglas. Two copies should be on board of the Andromeda project, with two additional copies of Vril 1.

*Leich bewapphete flugscheibe Vril 2

*Diameter : 10.50m

*Motor : Schuman-levitators

*Driver : Mag-yeld-impulser 3b

*Velocity : 6.000km/h (theoretically up 24.000km/h)

*Armament : Canons 1 x 80mm KSK on rotationg turret ; machines gun 2 x MK-108

*Shielding : Double Victalen

*Crew : 2 humans.

*Duration of stable fly : 12 minutes, day and night and all weather conditions.

*First Fly : 1942

*Date of running or working : 1944

VRIL 3 (1938):

The Vril 3 is a more powerful version of the Vril 2, and equipped with a canon.

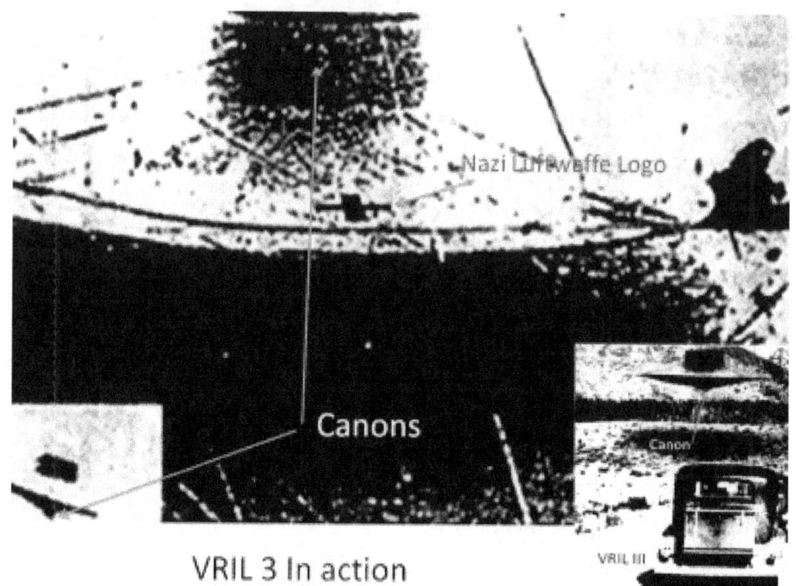

VRIL 3 In action

*Leich bewapphete flugscheibe Vril 3

*Diameter : 10.50m

*Motor : Schuman-levitators

*Driver : Mag-yeld-impulser 3b

*Velocity: 6.000km/h (theoretically up 24.000km/h)

*Armament: Canons 1 x 80mm KSK on rotating turret; machine guns 2 x MK-108 ; canon 1 x 75mm on rotating turret on the cockpit

*Shielding : Double Victalen

*Crew : 2 humans

*Duration of stable fly : 12 minutes, day and night in all weather conditions.

*First fly : 1943

*Date of running or working : 1944

VRIL 4 (1940) :

The Vril 4 comprises a tube above the cockpit mostly used as a magnifier otherwise, it is a variant of the Vril 2 and 3. It's always Shauberger team which is responsible for its design and development.

*Leich bewapphete flugscheibe Vril 4

*Diameter : 10.50m

*Motor : Schuman-levitators

*Driver : Mag-yeld-impulser 3b

*Velocity: 6.000km/h (theoretically up 24.000km/h)

*Armament: Canons 1 x 80mm KSK on rotating turret; machine guns 2 x MK-108

*Shielding : Double Victalen

*Crew : 2 humans

*Duration of stable fly: 12 minutes, day and night in all weather conditions.

*First fly: 1943

*Date of running or working: 1944

VRIL 5 (1942)

The Vril 5 is probably the most successful prototype for Schauberger team. From these first flights in 1944, it reached a speed of 12.000 km / h and it even seems that the craft has left the terrestrial atmosphere several times, with few trips into orbit.

With the Vril 5 the Nazis traveled to the moon and Mars and constructed secret bases and also traveled to the stars that are far from us three light years and more like the Aldebaran star in the constellation of Taurus. In the early 40s, it was possible to make color photographs. Here is the first dish of the Reich in color, the Vril 5.

Canon 1 x 75 mm On turret
Of The Cockpit
VRIL 5 On Ground
Some
Haunebu
& Vril
Cockpit
Interior
Design
Windows

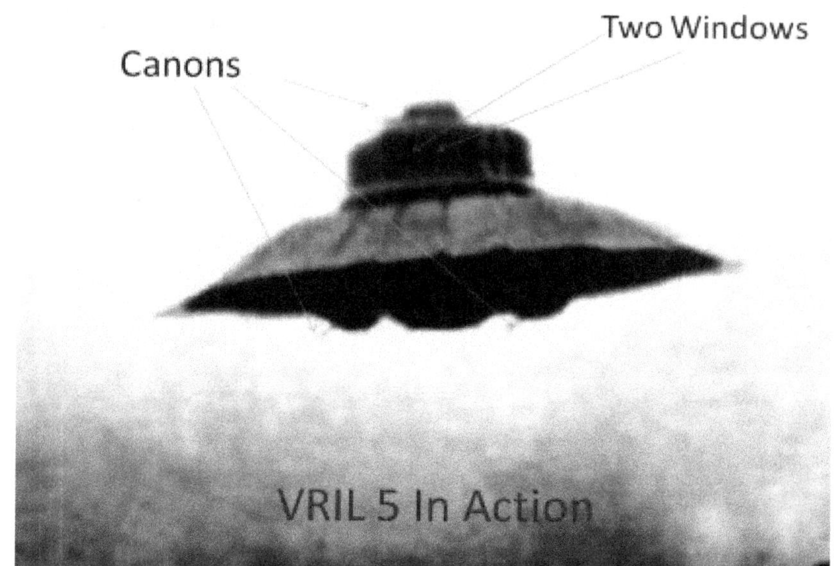
Canons
Two Windows
VRIL 5 In Action

*Leich bewapphete flugscheibe Vril 5

*Diameter: 10.5 meter.

*Motor: Thule Tachyonator (Triebwerk) 7b

*Drive: Mag-yeld-impulser 3c

*Velocity: 12.000km/h (theoretically up 48.000km/h).

*Armament: Canons 1 x 80mm KSK on rotating turret, machine guns 2 x MK-108, canon 1 x 75 mm on turret on the cockpit

*Shielding: Victalen triple

*Crew: 3 humans.

*Duration of stable fly: unknown

*First fly: 1944

VRIL 6 (1944)
*Leich bewapphete flugscheibe Vril 6
*Date of running or working: 1945

V 6 AND NAZIS PLANES

VRIL 7 (1944)

It was a project of giant vessels with 120 meters in diameter. The clear photo is from a Nazi long record of landing of Vril 7 then the RFZ 6 series' version UFO:

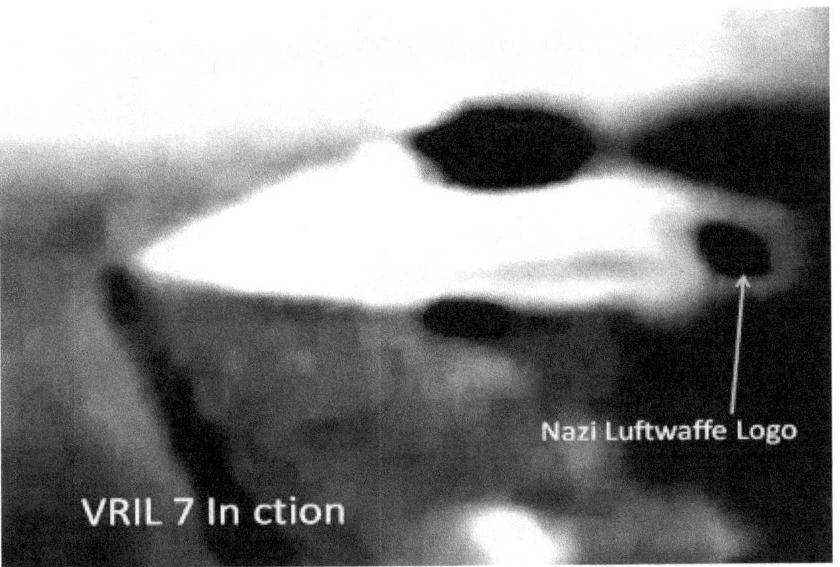
Nazi Luftwaffe Logo
VRIL 7 In ction

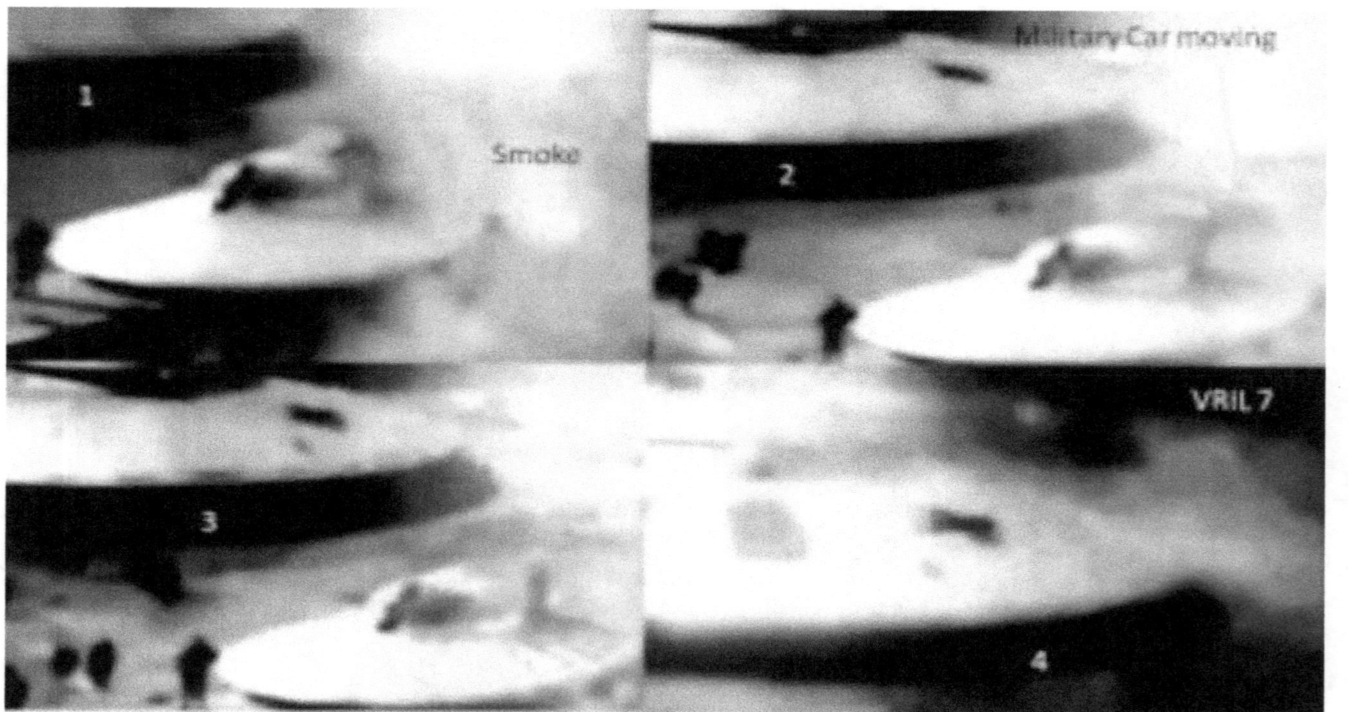

This sequence of photos is coming from a Nazi original film .The Vril 7 is alredy on gound then landed the RFZ 6 UFO version with the smoke form of the sand's ground(1).The people are moving to her as they were waiting for her.A military car moves in the (2).This is the best resolution for the images.

The Third Reich collaborated with Japan and gave to Mitsubishi at the time a V 7 to equip it with a Japanese engine.

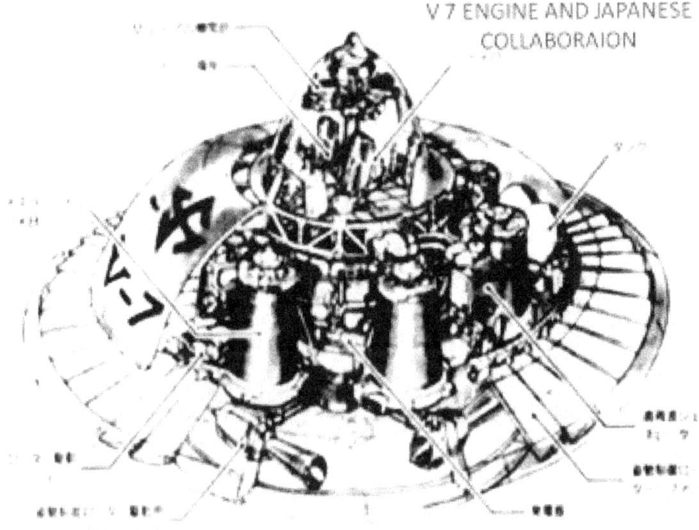

VRIL 8 (1945)

The Vril 8 "odin" built despite the end of the war.

* Leich bewapphete flugscheibe "odin" Vril 8

* Seen flying in 1946.

A datasheet presents an internal technical composition for a VRIL 8(ODIN):

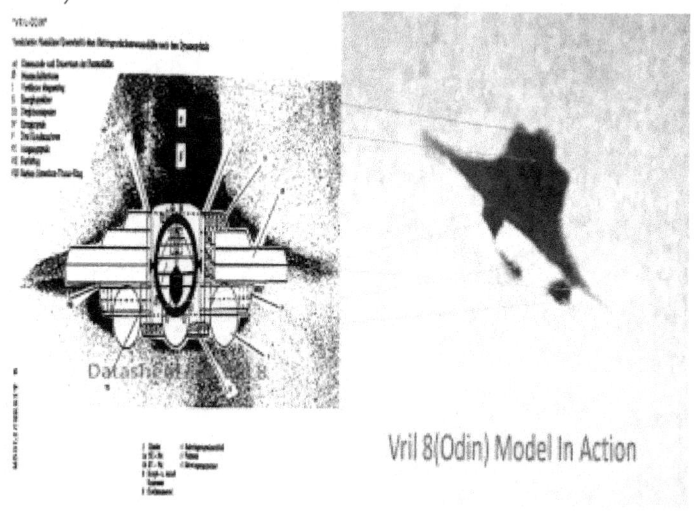

VRIL 9 (1945)

As many others built after the world War II.

* Leich bewapphete flugscheibe Vril 9

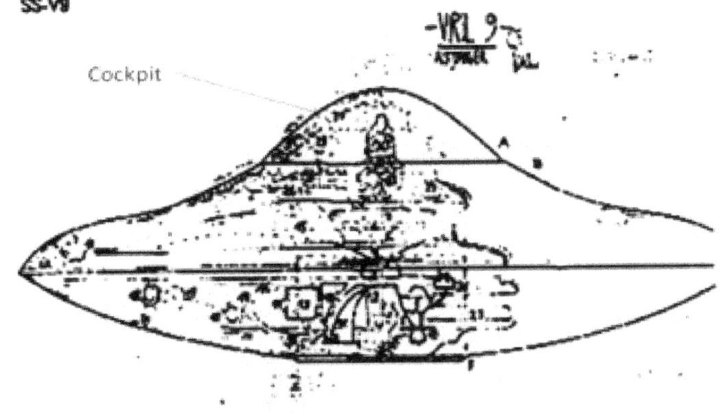

VRIL 9 Original Datasheet

* Seen Flying

in 1947, however there's a technical draw from the SS.

We must also take in consideration that the Vrils were used by the Aryans (Pure race) to displacement and movement.

VRIL 10(1944)

It has three machine Guns and one canon in the cockpit turret.

VRIL 11(1944)
Larger cockpit and a new addition upon it.

VRIL 11 with some modifications

VRIL12:

Just some modifications in the canons sizes and emplacements.

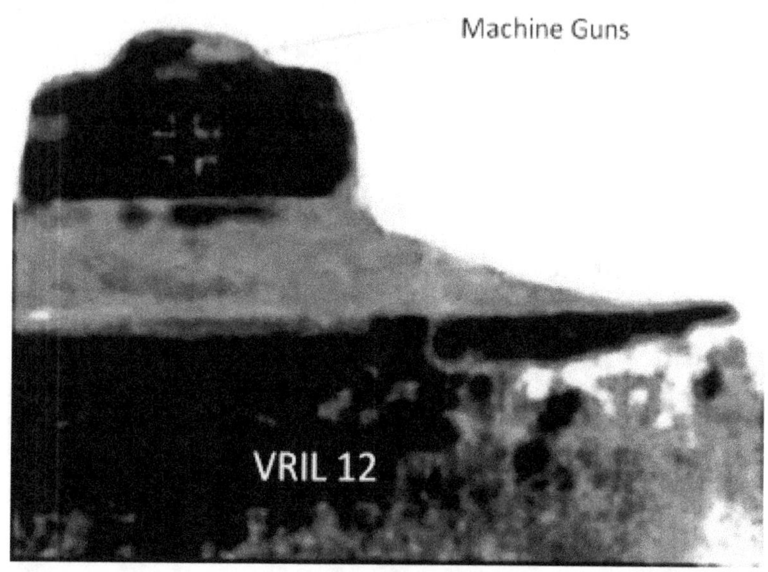

VRIL 13 :

It has a new concept of machine guns invented by Nazis. This machine gun has three vertical lined exits for a sized ammunition .It has too a heavy canon in the other side of the cockpit designed to target bombers.

VRIL 13 In Action

VRIL 14 :

VRIL 20:

Designed to the transportation of high official rankings of the Nazis elites.

Andromeda Project

The project Andromeda was designed by Hitler to make long distances travels in the universe. Its length varies between 139 and 300 meters, long cylindrical form or cigar, which may explains the multiple sightings of this vessel type, believing that it is an extraterrestrial origin and not human origin one.

With this machine, the Nazis have traveled up to 500 light years from earth and even reached the constellation of Taurus and precisely to the star Aldebaran .This craft can carry several other flying objects such as the type Haunebu, Vril or with other forms of gear as shown in the design of the secret datasheet below.

The plan for 1943 was to create a "mother" ship, with hangars for other "flying discs". The ship had about 30 meters in diameter, with a hangar for one device type Haunebu II, two VRIL-1 and two VRIL-2.

*Length : 139 m.

*Diameter : 30 m

*Motors : 4 * Thule tahyonatorem-11, 4 * Schumann-Levitator 16

*Driver: Mag-Field-Impulser, type 6b

*Velocity: 300 000 km / sec

*Duration of stable fly: theoretically unlimited

*Armament 2 * 2 * 110 m, 1 * 110 m 2 * 2 * 70, 4 * R100

*Crew: 130 persons

Andromeda have an "internal gravity", which allows the crew to feel comfortable at any position of the body, until overturned. The cigar form is one of the third Reich inventions with two figures: one a cylindrical and the other with a conical angle in the end of the flying saucer.

The cigar form also is a flying saucer from extraterrestrials coming from other worlds.

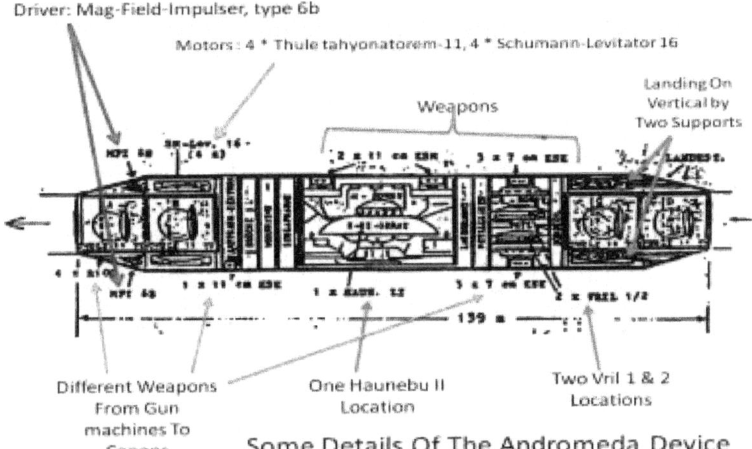

Some Details Of The Andromeda Device

An Original Datasheet For Andromeda Device From SS Archive Dated in December The 2nd, 1944

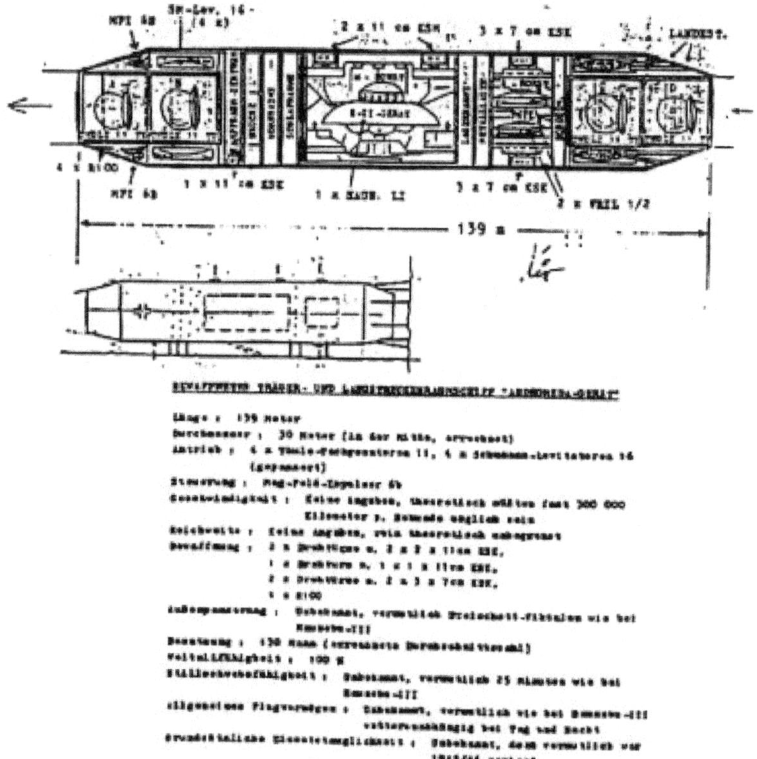

BEWAFFNETES TRÄGER- UND LANGSTRECKENRAUMSCHIFF "ANDROMEDA-GERÄT"

Länge : 139 Meter
Durchmesser : 30 Meter (in der Mitte, errechnet)
Antrieb : 4 x Thule-Tachyonatoren 11, 4 x Schumann-Levitatoren 16 (gepanzert)
Steuerung : Mag-Feld-Impulser 4b
Geschwindigkeit : Keine Angaben, theoretisch müßten fast 300 000 Kilometer p. Sekunde möglich sein
Reichweite : Keine Angaben, rein theoretisch unbegrenzt
Bewaffnung : 3 x Drehtürme m. 2 x 2 x 11cm KSK,
    1 x Drehturm m. 1 x 1 x 11cm KSK,
    2 x Drehtürme m. 2 x 3 x 7cm KSK,
    4 x 8100
Außenpanzerung : Unbekannt, vermutlich Freischütt-Fiktalen wie bei Kmasch-III
Besatzung : 130 Mann (errechnete Durchschnittszahl)
Feldtauglichkeit : 100 g
Stillstehschwebefähigkeit : Unbekannt, vermutlich 25 Minuten wie bei Kmasch-III
Allgemeine Flugvermögen : Unbekannt, vermutlich wie bei Kmasch-III wetterunabhängig bei Tag und Nacht
Grundsätzliche Einsatzmöglichkeit : Unbekannt, dem vermutlich vor 1945/46 geplant.
Beiboote : Q-Boot - 1 x Kmasch-II, B - Boot - 3 x Vril-1 , 2 x Vril-2

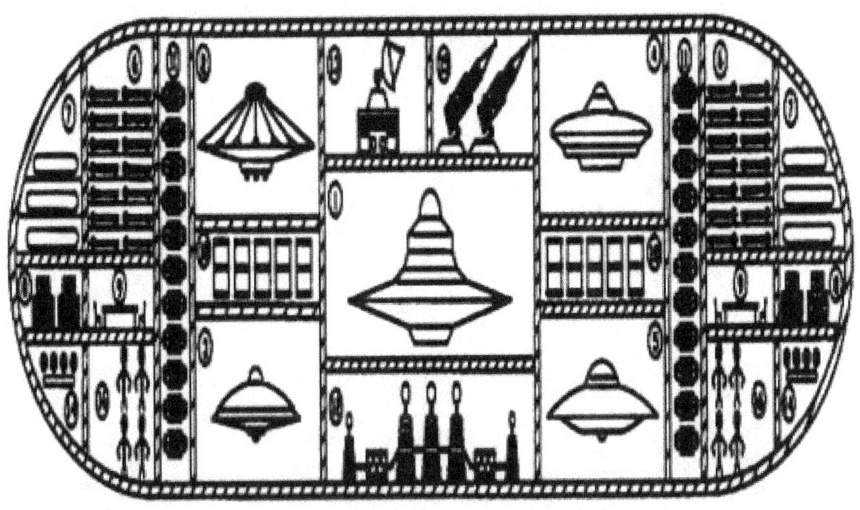

A Scheme For Andromeda Device Different departments

① FLUGALHAUFFEN
② SCHOONFRYDER
③ GOOGALSTIEN
④ KLIMENSCHTACH
⑤ SCHRAUSENHAU
⑥ SLEEPING QUARTERS
⑦ WATER SUPPLY
⑧ FOOD SUPPLY
⑨ BRIEFING ROOM
⑩ LIQUID MERCURY TANKS
⑪ ELECTRO-MAGNETIC INDUCERS
⑫ DRIVE UNIT/TESLA COILS
⑬ RADAR ROOM
⑭ INTER-PLANETARY SAMPLE STORAGE
⑮ WEAPONS SUPPLY
⑯ EXTRA-TERRESTRIAL DEBRIEFING ROOM

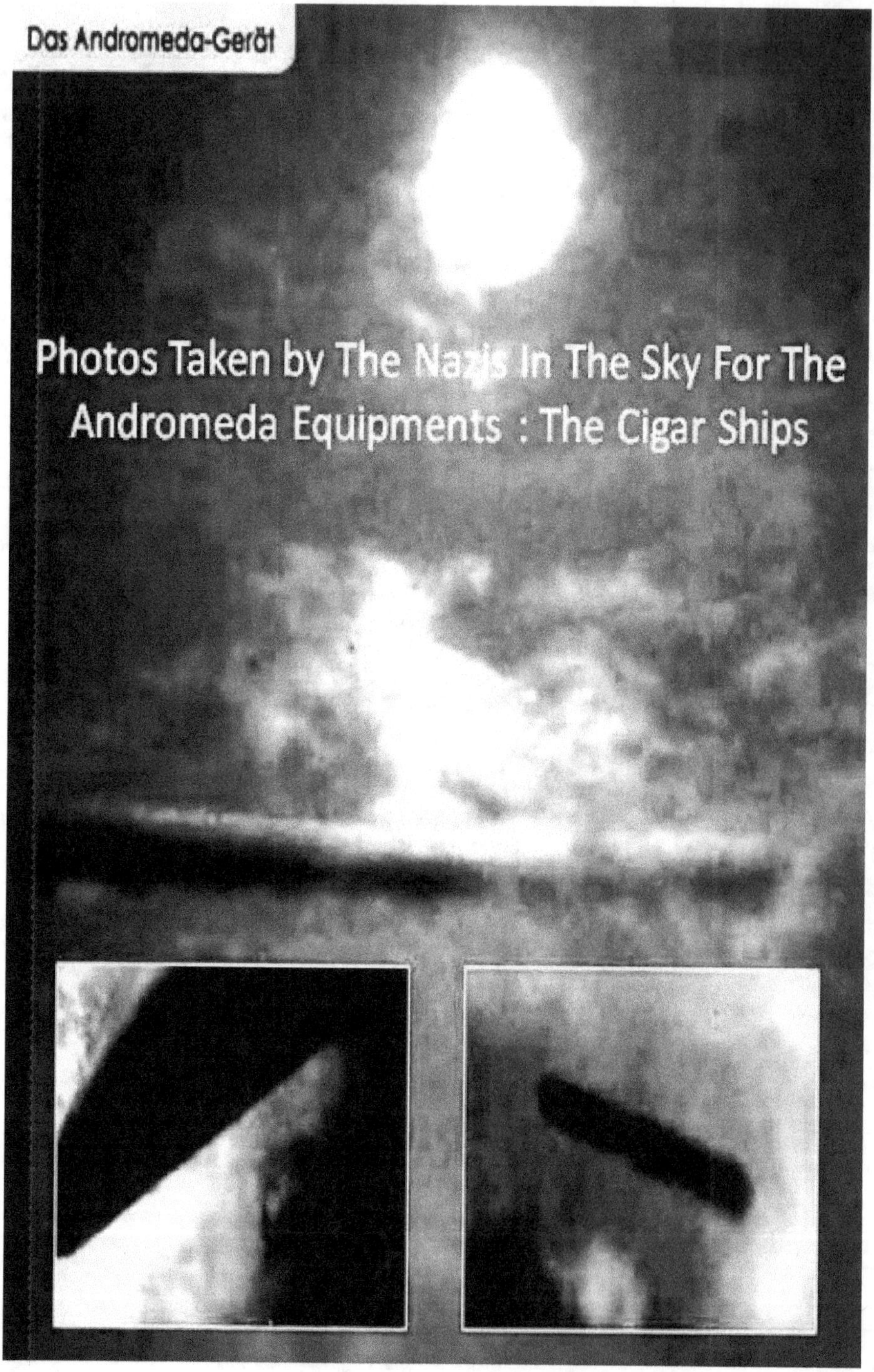

Das Andromeda-Gerät
Photos Taken by The Nazis In The Sky For The
Andromeda Equipments : The Cigar Ships
Das Andromeda-Gerät

Another Form Of
Andromeda Cigar Ships

The Conical Cigar Is another
Cigar Ship For Andromeda
Equipments

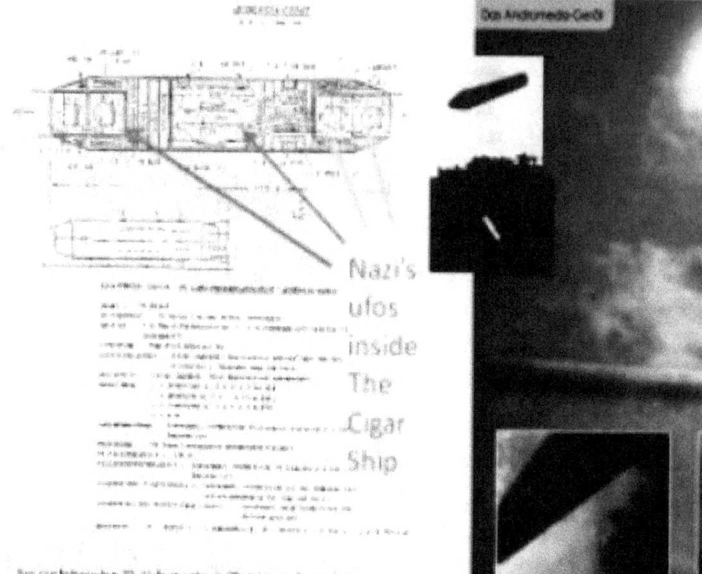

One Of Original Dataheets Designs
of Andromeda Project Cigar Ships

Original Photos of one of
Andromeda Project Cigar Ship

As I mentioned, before, the Nazis traveled to Aldebaran, Mars, moon and other planets and constellations and they met so many races of extraterrestrials. Perhaps, persons like George Adamski, could photographed with his modest telescope for so many times, Nazis flying saucers in front of the moon and nowadays, so many UFO investigators do the same thing.

An Original document for Mission Order to Aldebaran Star dated from March 1943:

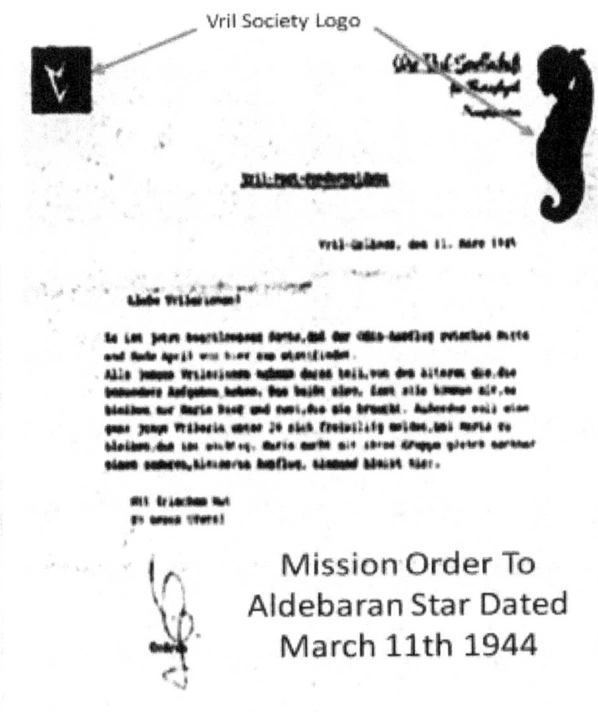

C.3: Proofs That Nazis UFOs still flying for 80 years Up Today.

To answer this question you should make a small comparison between the Nazis UFOs models like Vril, Haunibu and Andromeda with the modern sightings taken by amateurs smart phones and cameras worldwide.

You should take in consideration that their technology especially the external designs of flying saucers surely changed and developed over the time. We see planes, cars, trains and motorcycles designs evolved from the WWII until today so the same thing for the Nazis apparels that's why we see so many different designs in UFOs shapes from spherical to pyramidal to square to triangular to disc, etc.

Haunibu & Vril Models

A comparison between Haunibu I original design and a flying saucer caught over the snow in a winter of Switzerland shows a complete authenticity between the image and the Nazi's UFO datasheet .Despite this image is not really new but at least it was taken in the sixties of the twentieth century.

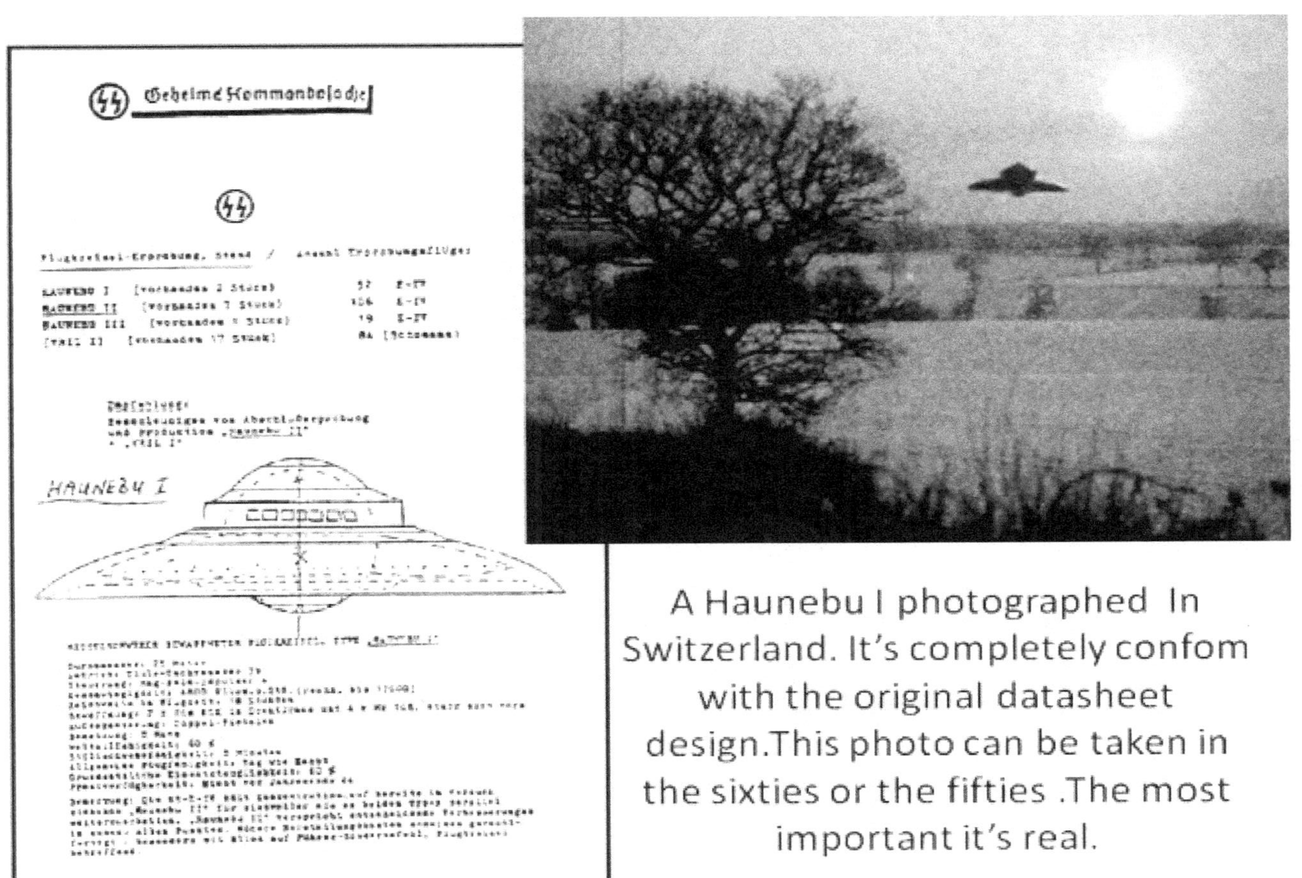

A Haunebu I photographed In Switzerland. It's completely confom with the original datasheet design.This photo can be taken in the sixties or the fifties .The most important it's real.

A comparison between a draft datasheet for Haunibu II model and an image of the same model flying saucer give approximately the same shape. Haunibu II datasheet was not leaked complete like the other ones in Haunibu series.

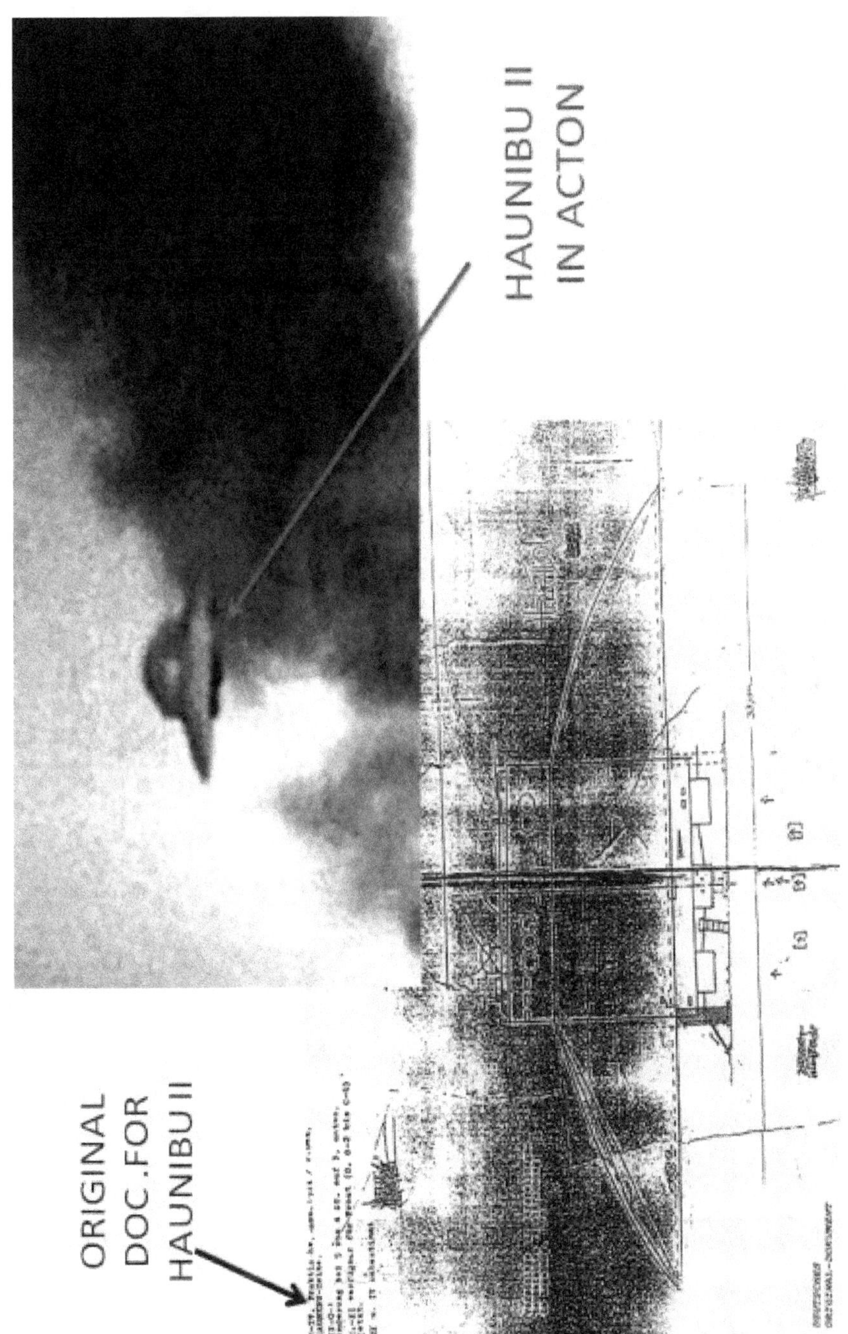
HAUNIBU II
IN ACTON
ORIGINAL
DOC. FOR
HAUNIBU II

A comparison between the Haunibu III original datasheet and the photos taken in different locations in the air and on the ground, reflects a typical authenticity in all the details.

Haunebu III Photographed By Nazis WithThe Presence Of Two Soldiers.

HAUNIBU III
MODEL

A comparison between the Haunebu IV model design and a photos of a UFO give a 100 % similarity between the two. Haunebu IV used and still used despite some sources claimed that this project unfinished.

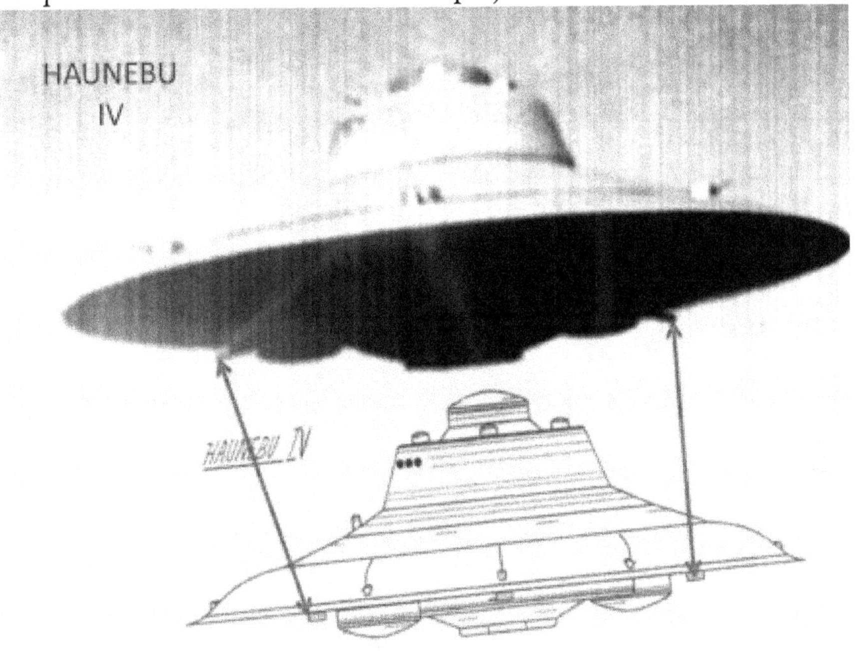

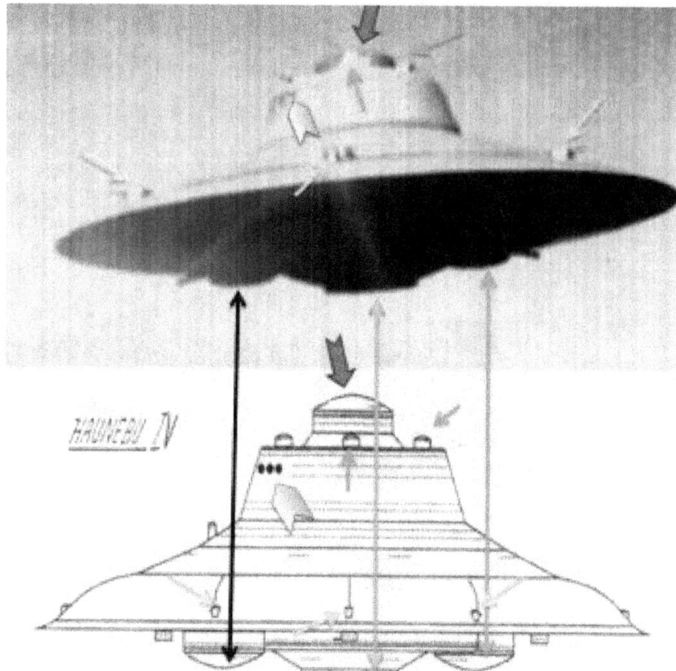

Complete Autenthicity between the Haunebu IV Datasheet Design and the image of a supposed Nazi's UFO.The diameter of this model is 120 meters.

A comparison between VRIL9 original datasheet design and a modern image taken from an amateur video in the twenty-first century shows a 90% similarity between them.

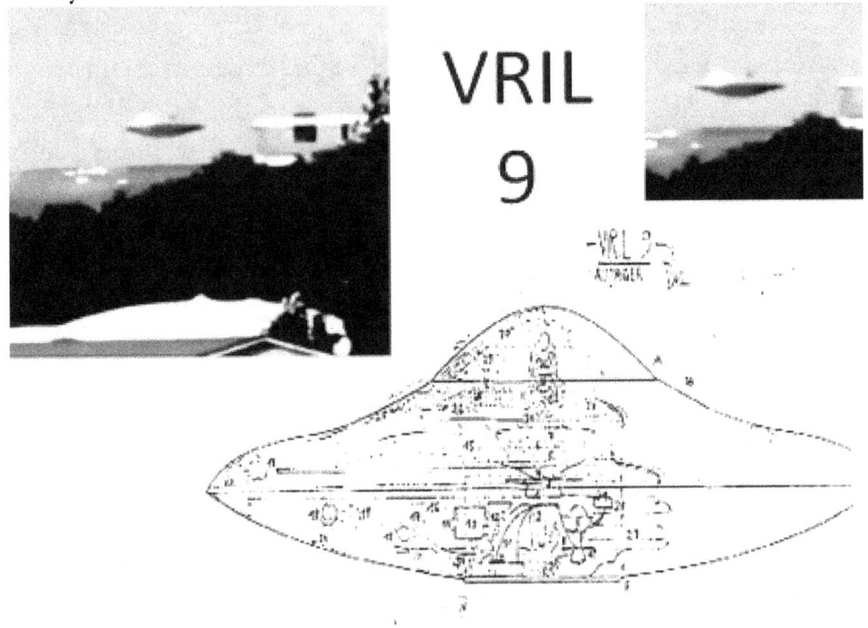

In 2012, a tourist recorded a video of two Nazi's flying saucers holding a cylindrical shape and spinning around it. The two UFOs were over the most famous pyramid of Mexico the Chichen Itza pyramid.

A comparison between the VRIL I original datasheet design with a white and black image for the same model we find a complete similarity with 100% .The VRIL I has a laser beam canon.Comparing both with the first UFO over Chichen Itza pyramid we find too a complete authenticity but with some little developments in the matter of the laser beam canon which became bigger with a bulb mostly processed with a technical glass and a harder cockpit glass.

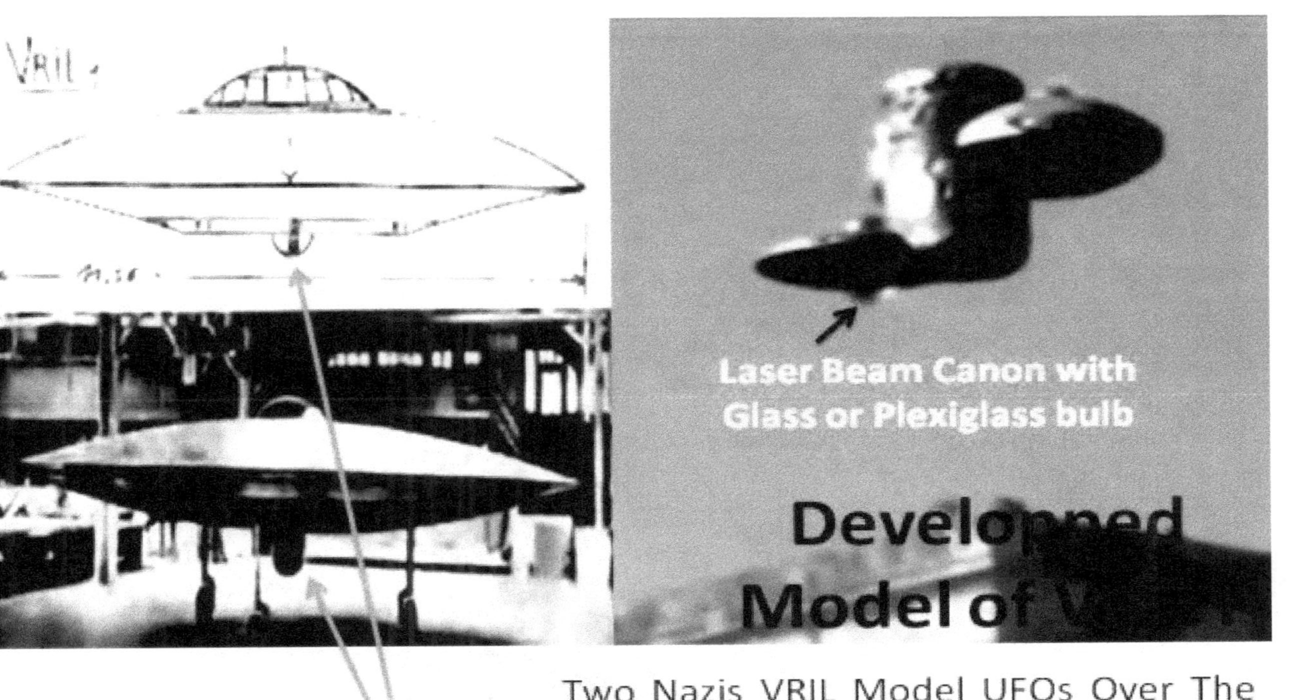

Two Nazis VRIL Model UFOs Over The Chicheen Itza Pyramid the most famous Temple in The Mayas Culture. Image from a Tourist video.

The same thing for the VRIL II Model, by comparing the original datasheet design and images taken in different locations I find a complete similarity with 100 % authenticity .The second Nazi's UFO over the Chichen Itza pyramid is too a developed Model for The VRIL II.

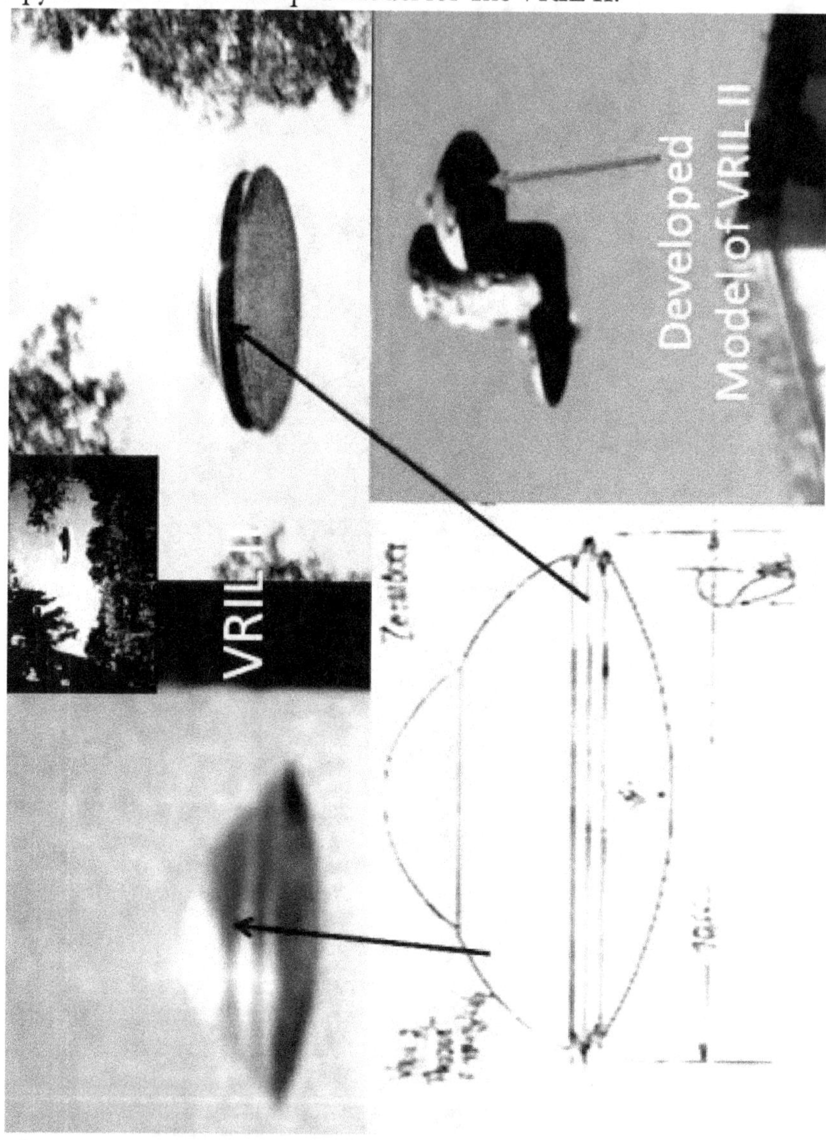

This is mosaic of captions taken from the original footage describing the scene presented by the two Nazi's Flying Saucers.

A comparison between an image taken from the leaked rare footage of the Nazis UFOs attack on US Naval Ships near Antarctica under the operation of High Jump led by Richard Byrd, shows typical design between this Nazi UFO and modern photos photographed in the twentieth century:

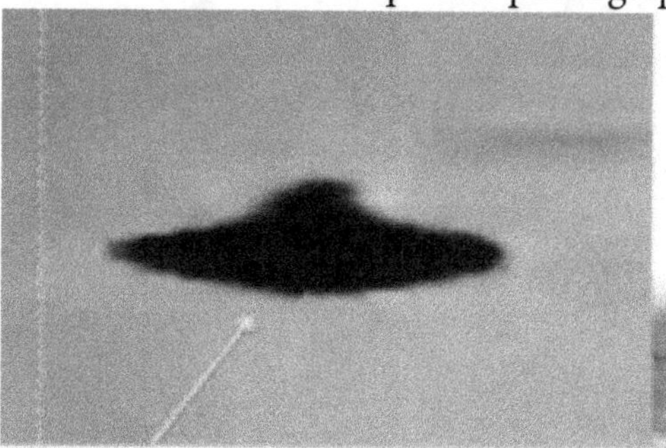

This image is taken from the leaked rare video of The Nazis UFOs attack to the High Jump Operation Ships near Antarctica it's the same like both modern photos of the Twentieth century.

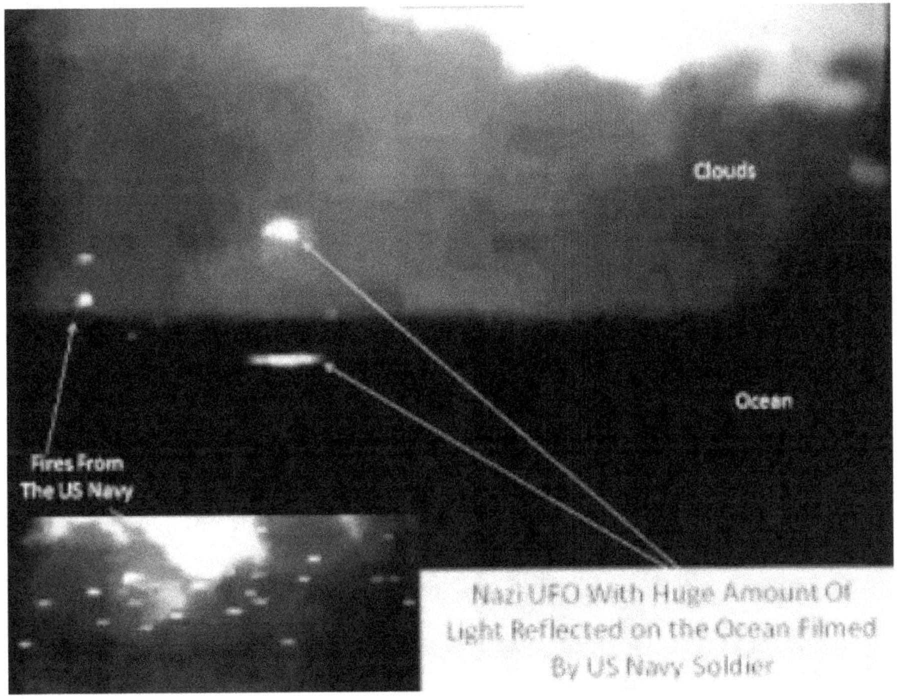

Nazi UFO With Huge Amount Of Light Reflected on the Ocean Filmed By US Navy Soldier

Also another proof That Nazis UFOs are real is the balls of light that people records worldwide are mostly the Nazis as they appeared in the High Jump videos and even the light reflected in the surface of the ocean followed by the fire balls of the US Naval:

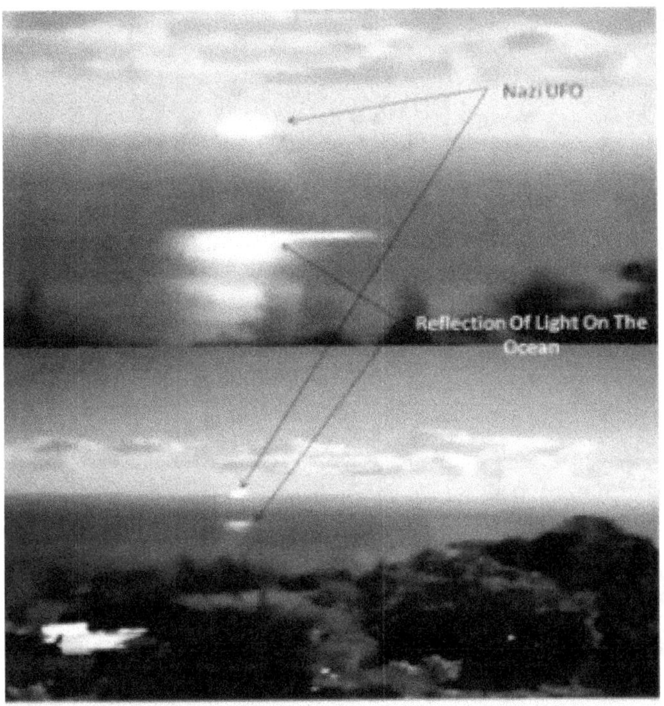

A Nazi UFO In The Form Of A Ball Of Light In
Hawaii Island In 2019

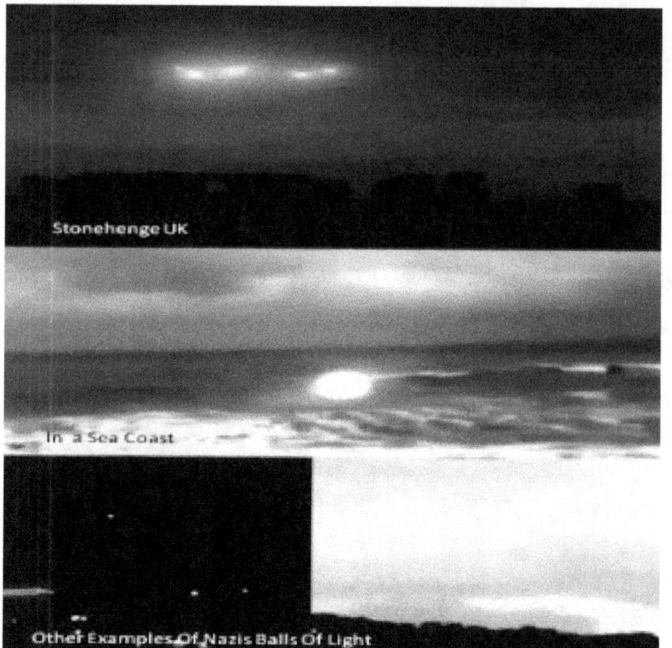
Stonehenge UK
In a Sea Coast
Other Examples Of Nazis Balls Of Light

Andromeda Project Cigar Models

For the Cigar shape Nazi's UFOs, we need to make a simple comparison between the original datasheet design and the photos in a side and the modern images and footages recorded in the twenty-First century.

From the datasheet we see the Cigar shape Ship holding several types or Models of Flying Saucers.

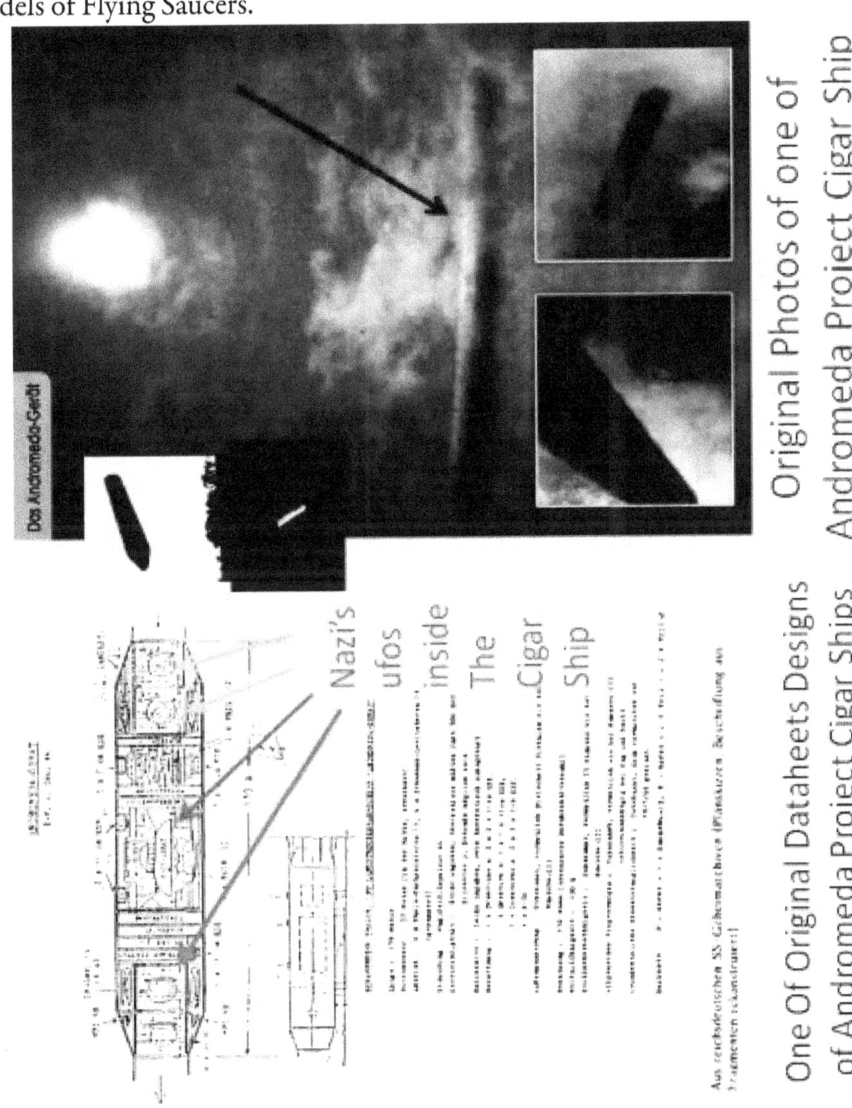

Original Photos of one of Andromeda Project Cigar Ship

One Of Original Dataheets Designs of Andromeda Project Cigar Ships

From a modern footage we have here a Cigar shape Flying Saucer and two UFOs waiting for this Cigar to come and took them. The two UFOs took their positions to enter to this Flying Saucer.

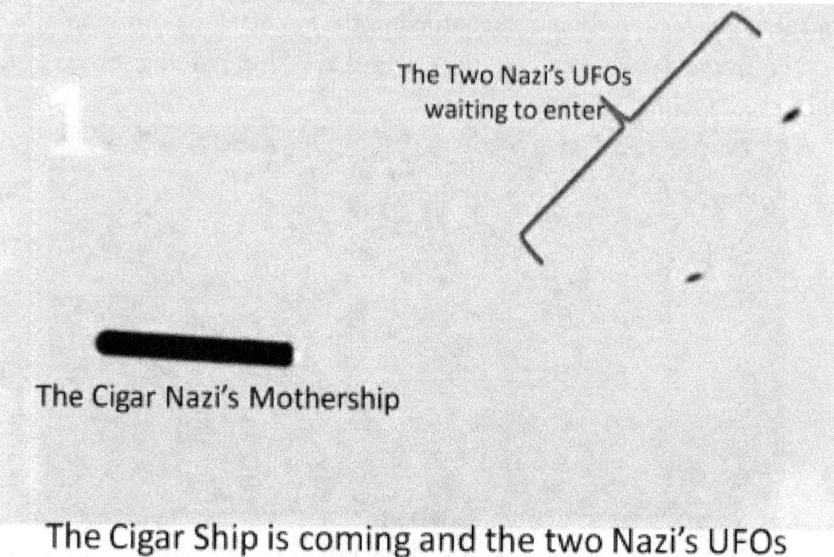

The Cigar Ship is coming and the two Nazi's UFOs already waiting are ready to enter to this Nazi's mothership

The first UFO moves to enter to the first door or portal as we see in these sequences.

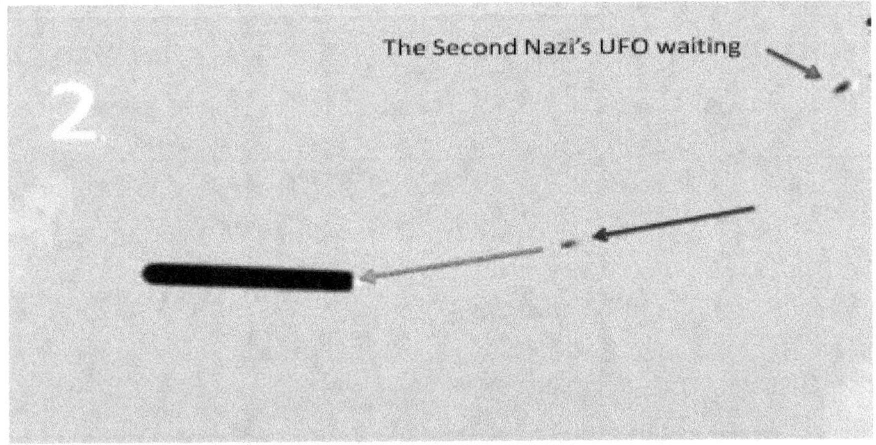

The First Nazi's UFO moves to enter to the first Door of the Cigar Mothership

The first UFO entered while the second one waits for his turn.

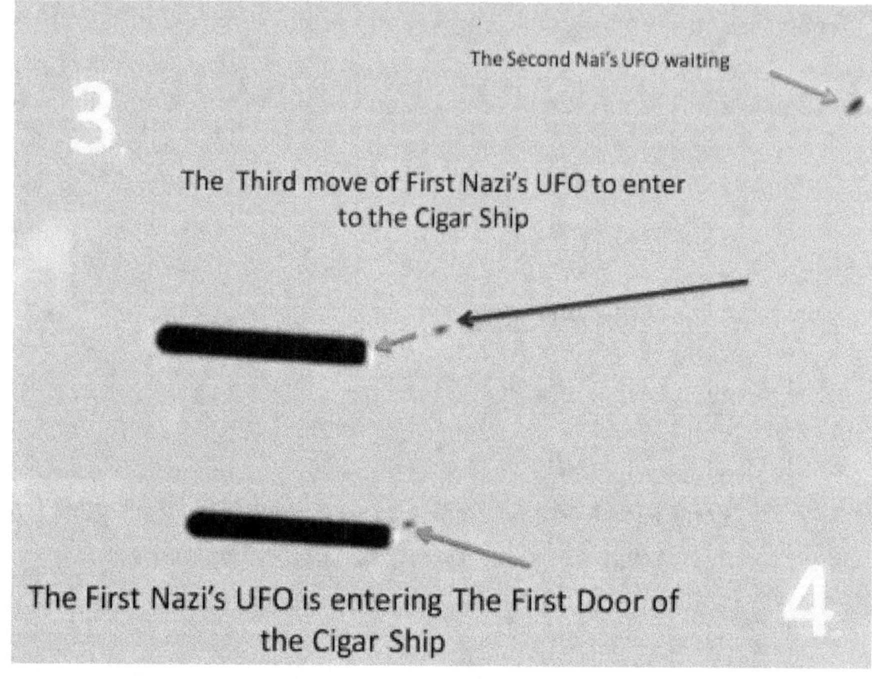

In these sequences, the second UFO moves to the second door of the Cigar Ship. By an instant sight to the original datasheet we see two UFOs side by side one enter by a first door and other by a second door. Something confirming the authenticity between them and the clear statement to declare which is the Nazis are alive and their UFOs are still flying and developed too but mainstream media ignore this matter intentionally and show it as a Myth.

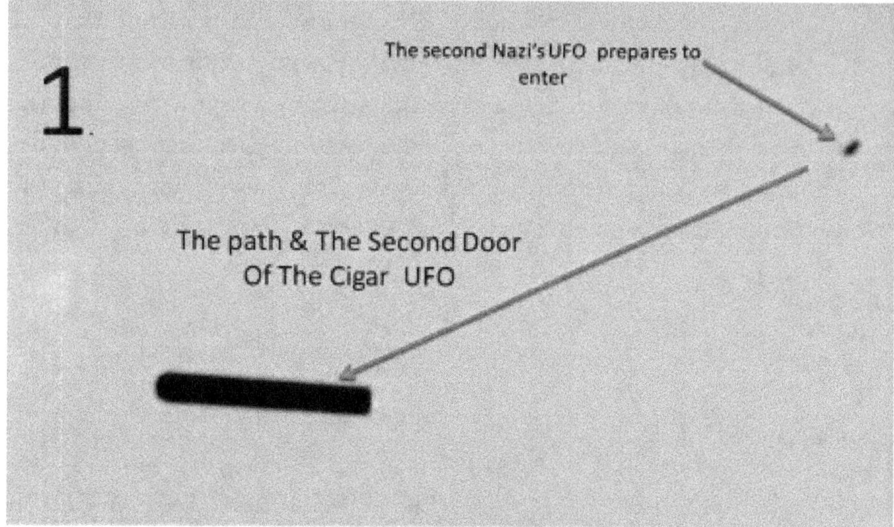

The second Nazi's UFO waits to enter to the Cigar Shape UFO after the enter of the first one

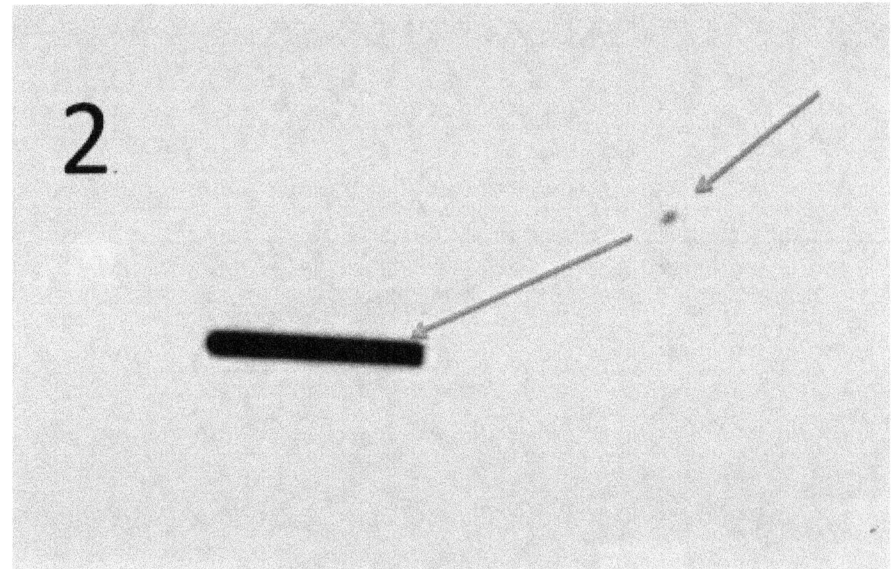

The second Nazi's UFO moves to enter to the Cigar Shape UFO after the enter of the first one

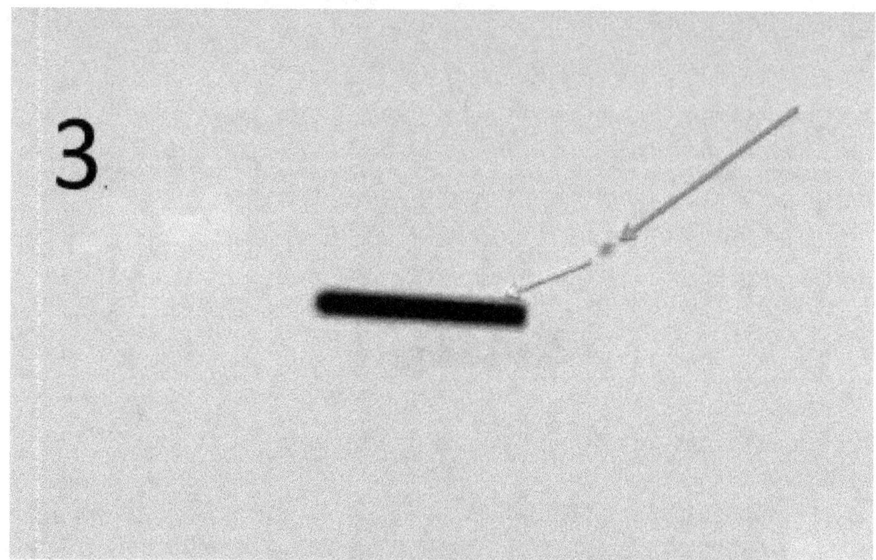

Third Caption for the move of the second Nazi's
UFO To the Cigar Shape UFO

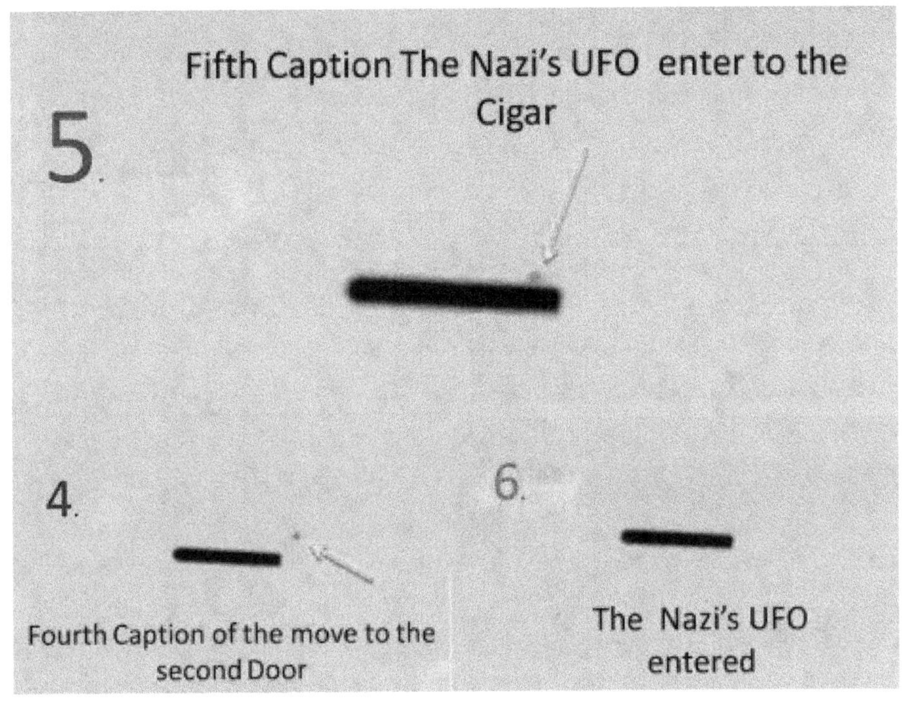
Fifth Caption The Nazi's UFO enter to the
Cigar
5.
4.
6.
Fourth Caption of the move to the
second Door
The Nazi's UFO
entered

Black color due to the Sun
Shadow and the far distance of
the UFO

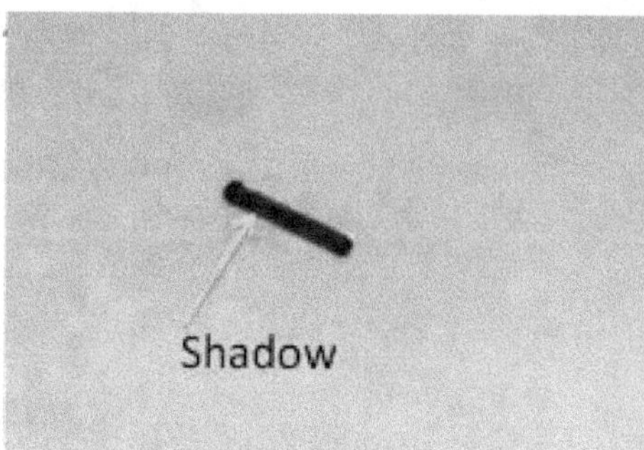

The Same Cigar Ship but the shadow make it black when it changes
direction the shadow goes and the appearence changes too

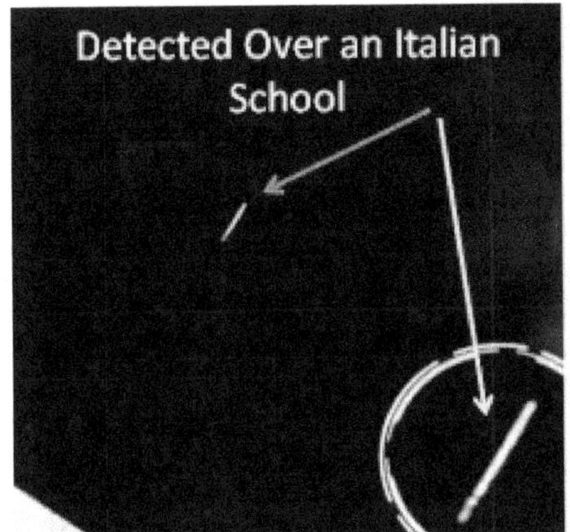

Some other Cigar
Ships detected
worldwide with
alternative forms

C.4: The Nazis & Their UFOs Where Are They Now?

The first nearest place is in Antarctica .In 1944 a message sent by a Nazi's Submarine claiming that they discovered huge caves under Antarctica and another land next to Antarctica after a long voyage in a long 1200 km cave.

This reinforce the theory that they have secret bases under the Antarctica mainland can be acceded just by Submarines and Sea UFOs .In 1943, the Nazi Admiral Karl Donitz declared: "The German Submarine Fleet is proud of having built for the Fuhrer in another part of the world a Shangri-La on land, an impregnable Fortress...".This Declaration confirms that The Nazis existence wasn't finished in the World War Two as the so called modern Historians told us via their Books and Documentaries.

C.5: The Continent After Antarctica

The second place is the land After Antarctica which is not mentioned today by the mainstream geography and science community, ignored completely by Google earth and maps and all the documentaries, series, cartoon and movies produced after the world war two until today!

In a Television Interview for the Admiral Richard Evelyn Byrd made in CBS station in 1954 for a program called: Longines Chronosope .The CBS correspondent at that time Larry Lesueur asked him : *"...Is already unexplored land left on this earth that might appeal to adventurers young Americans..?"* Admiral Richard Byrd answered:

" Yes there's and not up around the North Pole because it's getting credit up there because they find out it's really usable not only to live in but militarily *but strangely enough there's left in the world today an area as big as United States that's never been seen by human being and that's beyond the Pole on the other side of the South Pole from Middle America...And I think it's a quiet astonishing it should be an area as big as unexplored so a lot of Adventures left done at the bottom of the world*

Kenneth Crawford (a Newsweek Magazine Editor):*"Well would you hope to see that?"*.

Admiral Byrd: *"I do"* (laughing).

You should ask here: where is this unexplored land in Google earth and maps applications? Why we don't see it in the world map? Where are the so called scientific communities? Where are the geologists, the geographers worldwide? Where is NASA and her little sisters space Agencies from Europe, UK, Japan, Brazil, Russia and China?

Does Admiral Richard Byrd was wrong the renowned person in exploration! The answer is this continent exist and other continents too .So the Nazis at least and primarily are based on this virgin continent built a new unnamed country and unknown for all the humanity.

They built an entire new civilization and here you can ask yourself how it can be this civilization especially when we know that they use the flying saucers and cigar shape airships not normal planes like we have, think about their cars, their cities, etc it's like one of future cities presented to us from Hollywood but it's already existed from 70 years ago at least.

Admiral Richard Byrd died in 1957 two years after this interview with a heart failure mostly the cause was a killing crime for me.

In 1961 an international agreement was signed between USA and many other countries to not send military equipments or personals to Antarctica and any expedition should take the pass to go there and should give her detailed plan of the visit previously.

Think for a minute, the Nazis are there for most than 80 years now in a huge continent how is their lives, how did they developed their technologies for all this period of time Why the mainstream media ignored them and why they didn't destroy the USA in world war two and after as the USA was the ultimate cause of third Reich defeat? What's about the testimony of Admiral Richard Byrd the well known and recognized Explorer by the entire USA from normal people to militaries to scientists?

People are not aware that most UFOs sightings showing cigar shapes and other shapes are Nazis and they do this to program them that there's a potential danger from Extraterrestrials, they'll still do this until the due date

The images below are from a Nazi short movie for a Mammoth filmed in Antarctica as it's not entirely discovered until today with 14 millions square kilometers or in the land after Antarctica. Remark here for the modern humans and the so called scientific community the Mammoth is extinct but just in the five known continents not in the other ones(our supposed known world)!

A Mammoth Filmed By A Nazi In Antarctica Or
In The Land After Antarctica

C.6: Volcanoes Craters, Mountains & Seas

So many times when Nazis UFOs were seen entering active volcanoes craters from the disc shape ones to the cigar shape ones. We have here two scenarios, the first one is the Nazis have secret tunnels bases on these volcanoes but we should ask here does the bases and the UFOs has sophisticated materials insulation for the heat of these volcanoes?

The second scenario is that the Nazis UFOs needs some heat or any ingredient in the composition of the volcano smoke to recharge their mechanism systems or use this smoke in their secret projects. Furthermore they do this for the show to make people thinking that they are extraterrestrials.

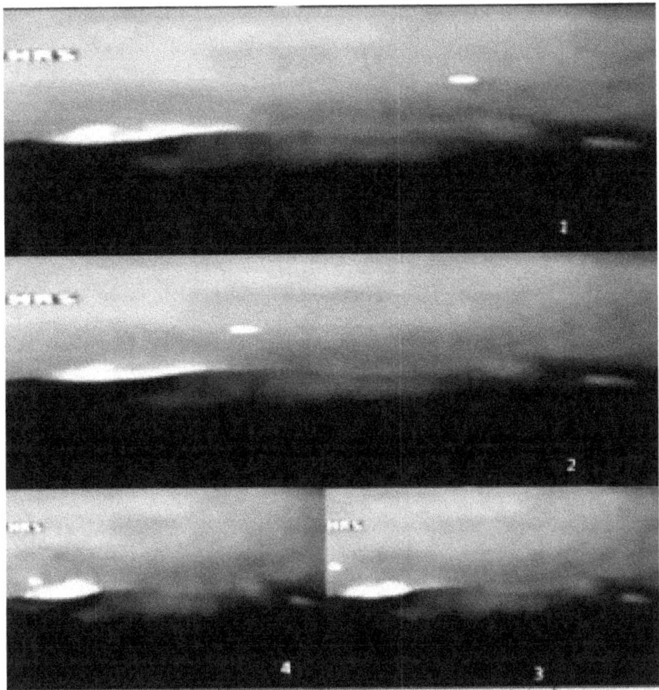

A Nazi UFO Enter To An Active Volcano
Crater

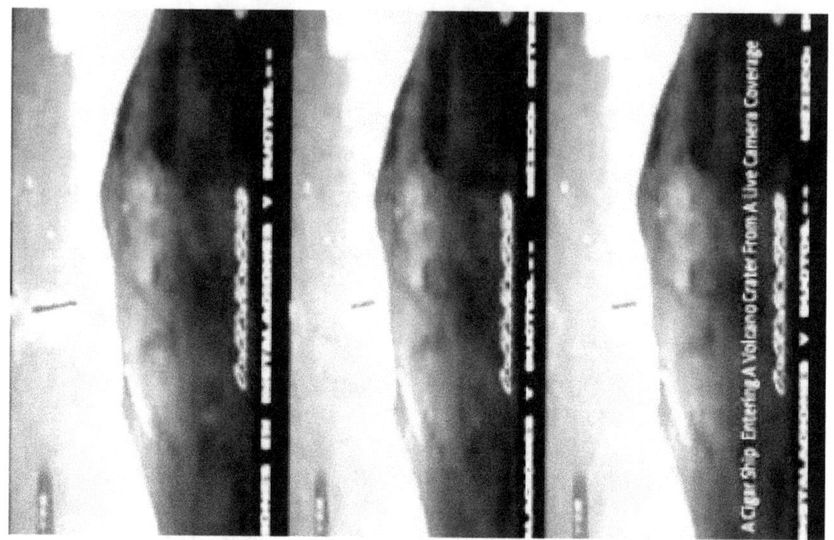
A Cigar Ship Entering A Volcano Crater From A Live Camera Coverage

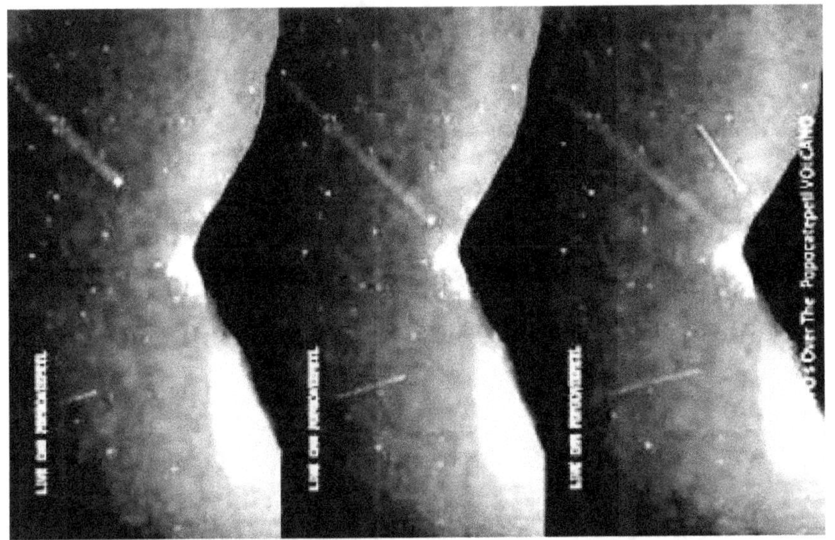
UFO Over The Popocatpetl Volcano

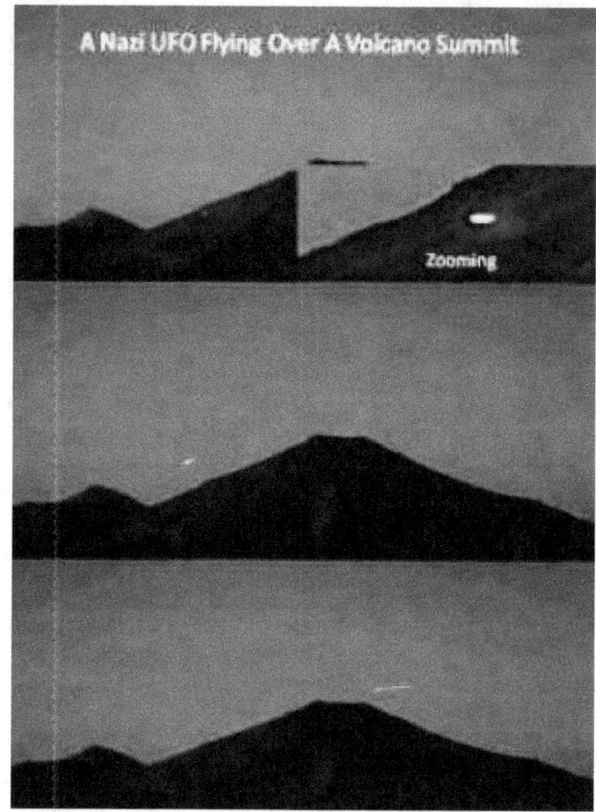
A Nazi UFO Flying Over A Volcano Summit
Zooming
A Nazi UFO Flying Over A Volcano Summit

They have too bases in the oceans and seas the proof that they emerged from the ocean when they attacked High Jump operation ships in 1947 and the modern sightings of the UFOs seen emerges and enter to the water this reinforce the theory that those UFOs engines works with water and this is cannot be strange as we have cars working with water not fuel the oil corporations can't leave this spread worldwide. As a modern example a Nazi UFO submerged to the ocean in Spain Coast when it was followed by two military planes:

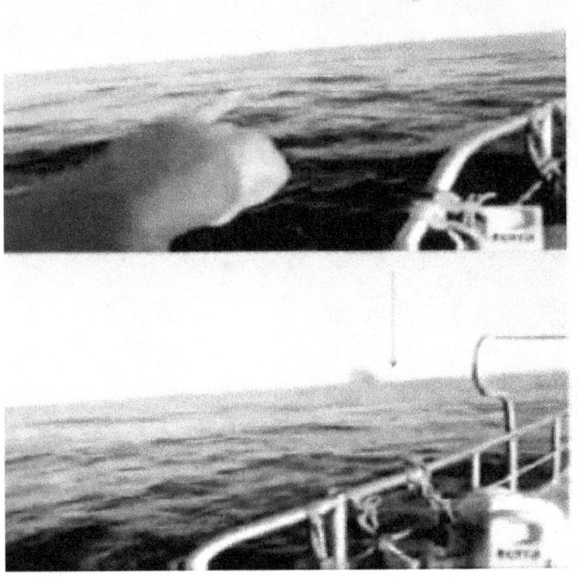

The Nazis UFOs use too bases on different mountains and deserts or any kind of ecosystems they use camouflage and this is clear in the colors of used UFOs. For example in a snowy mountains they use the white colored UFOs, in the desert they use the yellow ones and the brown ones for the desert brown mountains and even in Hawaii island they use the palms and herbs to cover the UFOs. These photos talks about this:

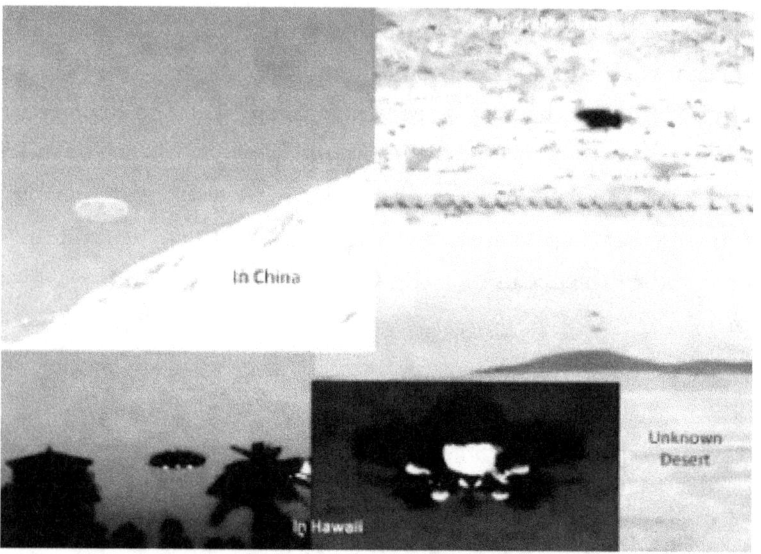
In China
Unknown
Desert
In Hawaii

C.7: The Dark Side Of The Moon

The dark side of the moon shows several structures and buildings belongs to so many civilizations leaked from the secret archives of Soviet Intelligence Service KGB and NASA.

This is for example a photo of a moon city's remains.

There are so many modern civilizations which enter and exit to and from the moon every day and with the architecture of homes that appears as parallel lines.

Zeeman Crater:

In deed one of landing sites on the moon for the US space program was on a crater field called: Zeeman crater, one of the shocking realities, that there are old houses of stones and wood, one of them has a width of 9 meters, a height of 6 meters and a length of sixty feet (18,3 meters) with 12 large doors. Those monuments are mostly former Nazis bases who have traveled to the moon around the year 1942.

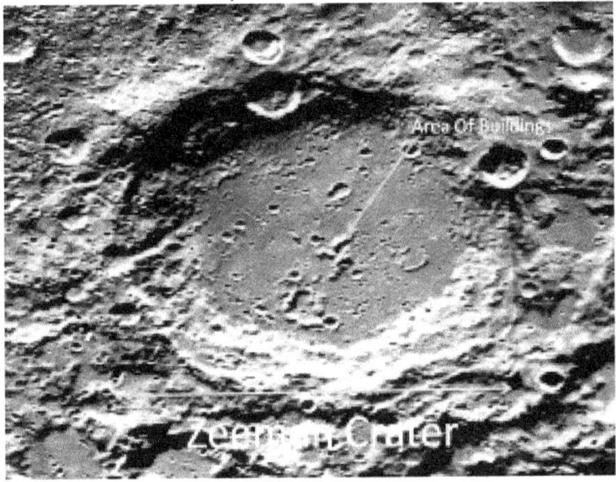

The photo below is for an Astronaut in front of underground concrete structure:

The Nazis were and still known as experts in Concrete Buildings especially in The Atlantic Wall multiple sites for the camouflaged huge canons or to resists to the allies huge bombs. This is increase the possibility of presence of Nazis on the moon and not be a myth.

The Nazi's Atlantic Wall is one of greatest proof of possibility of Nazis Buildings Capabilities in the Moon.

A huge concrete structure, compare its size with the astronaut:

One of such important discoveries on the moon is the existence of composition of the water: oxygen and hydrogen and also the nitrogen, important factors for the development of a life.

Another secret discovery but in the same time anyone on earth can see it on moon photos is an energy material mostly the Helium 3 that can replace oil and gas with a large difference in quality and quantity, this Helium is located in the south pole of the moon. But mainstream media don't talk about this.

This photo, shows the Helium 3 in South Pole of the moon and as you can see the light is very strong:

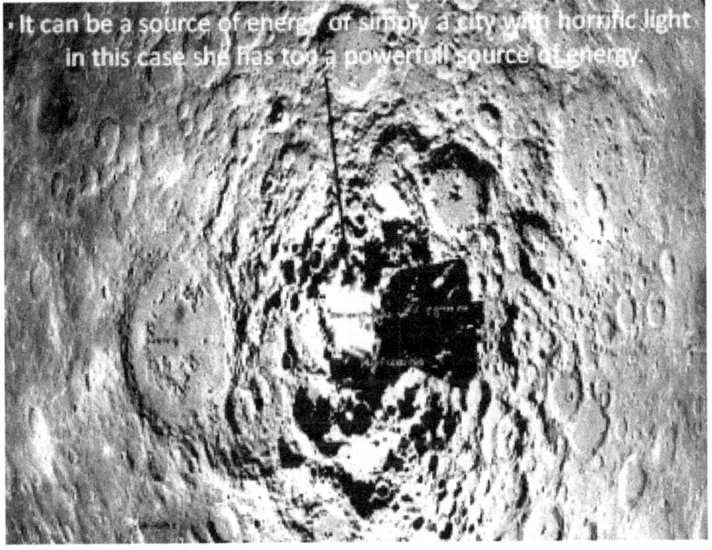

This source of energy is used by the inhabitants of the moon, from some races of extraterrestrials, the Nazis, Americans, Russians and Japanese, each of them has his proper territories that he defends and fights any external entries. This is very clear through the photos that coming from this planet from the sixties.

A huge Canon on top of a mountain mostly taken as a base from The Nazis

The huge Canon placed on the Top of an artificial base. This arm is very similar to the huge Nazis ones like Dora and Gustav canons used in World War II, these canons requires more than 3000 persons to be functional . What we see today in Germany is a continuation for the German traditional technology trends in the huge constructions machines .This reinforces the theory of the existence of Nazis in the moon.

The Helium 3 is used to construct huge structures and tours with the use of huge trucks, like this one:

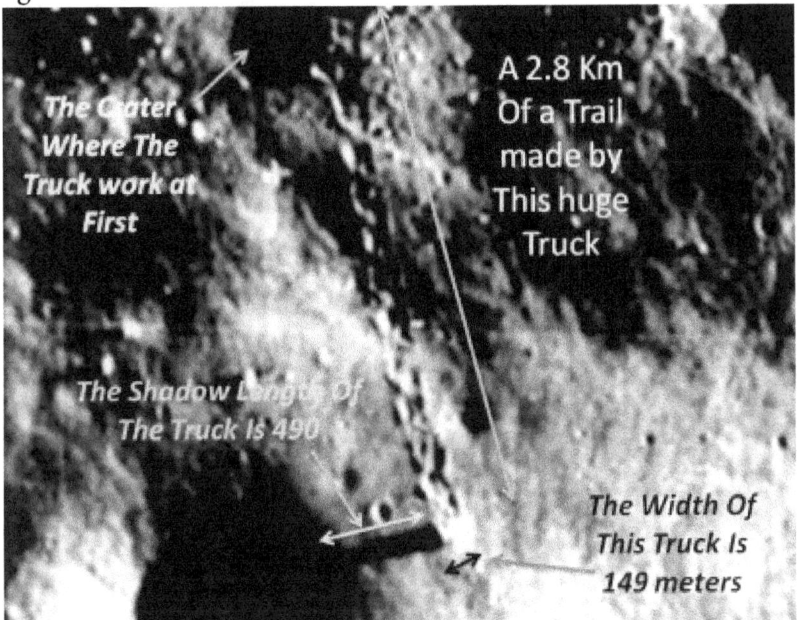

A huge mines truck leaving a crater and continued to roll, leaving a long trail behind him with distance of 2.8 km (9186 feet) .The width of the tractor is 149 meters(489 feet), leaving a height shadow of 490 meters(1607,5 feet). This explains the presence of towns and towers.

This tower for example has a height of 18 Km (59055 feet) taken by the Japanese probe Selene.

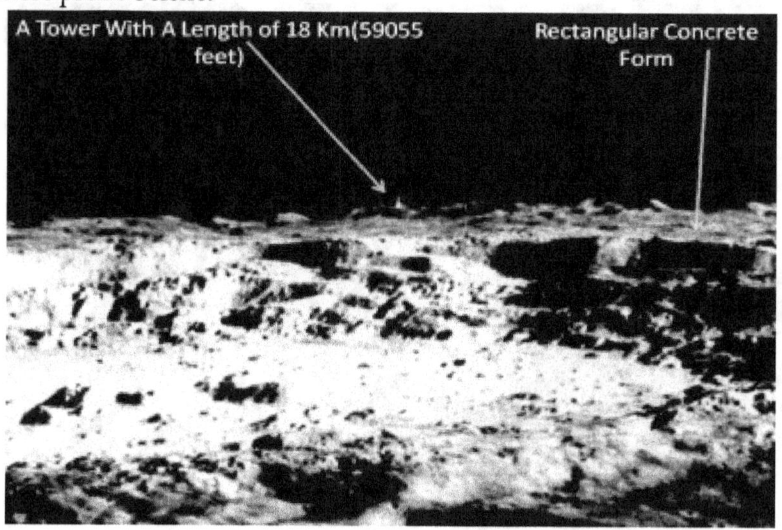

Other towers were erased by NASA, with its attempts to erase the truth and to cover it:

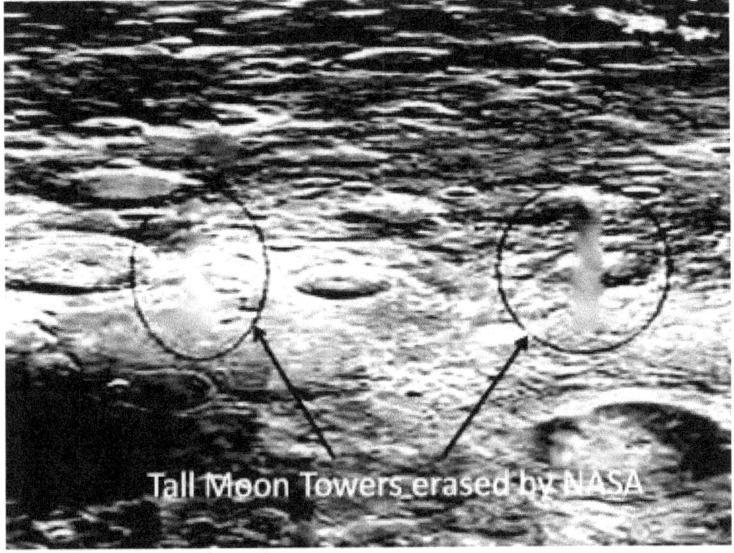

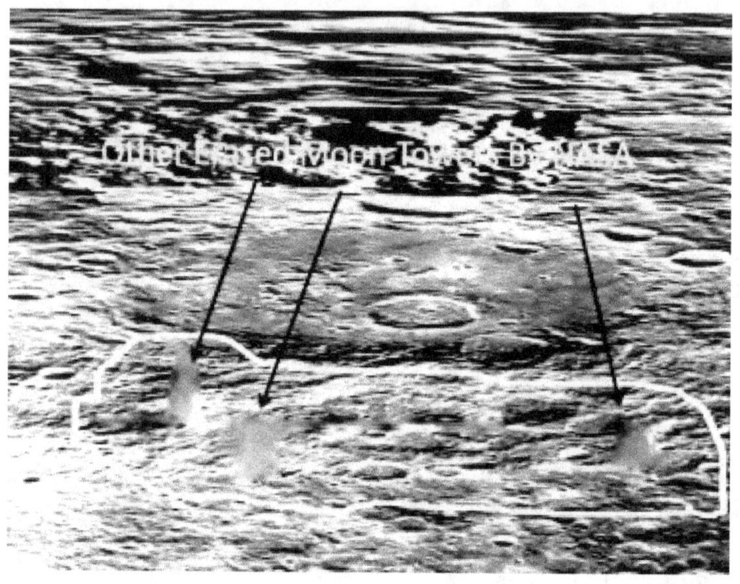
Other Erased Moon Towers By NASA

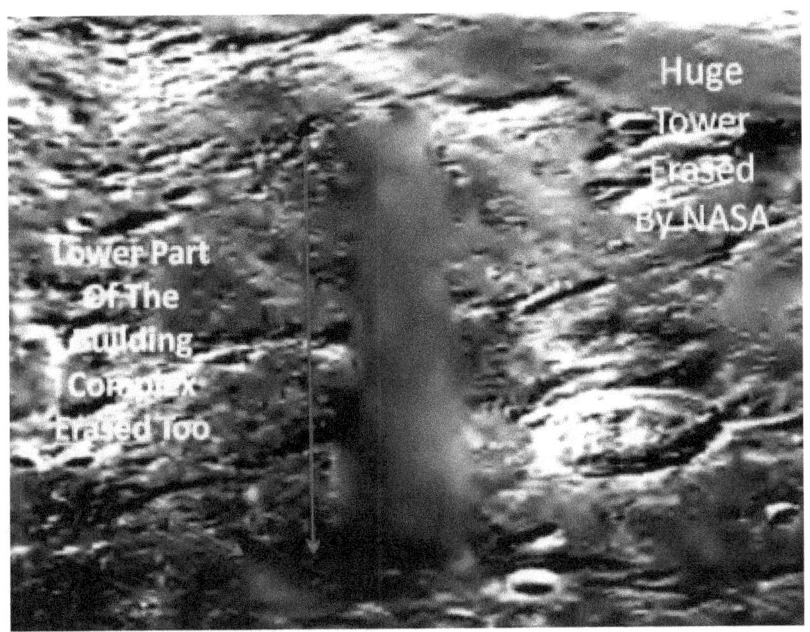
Huge
Tower
Erased
By NASA
Tower Part
Of The
Building
Complex
Erased Too

In the next image huge concrete complex habitations and installations inside an artificial rectangular crater .Next to it a natural circular crater .That gives an idea for the misinformation about the atmosphere, the moon gravity and else's gave by NASA her sisters and the so called scientific community which can be manipulated too

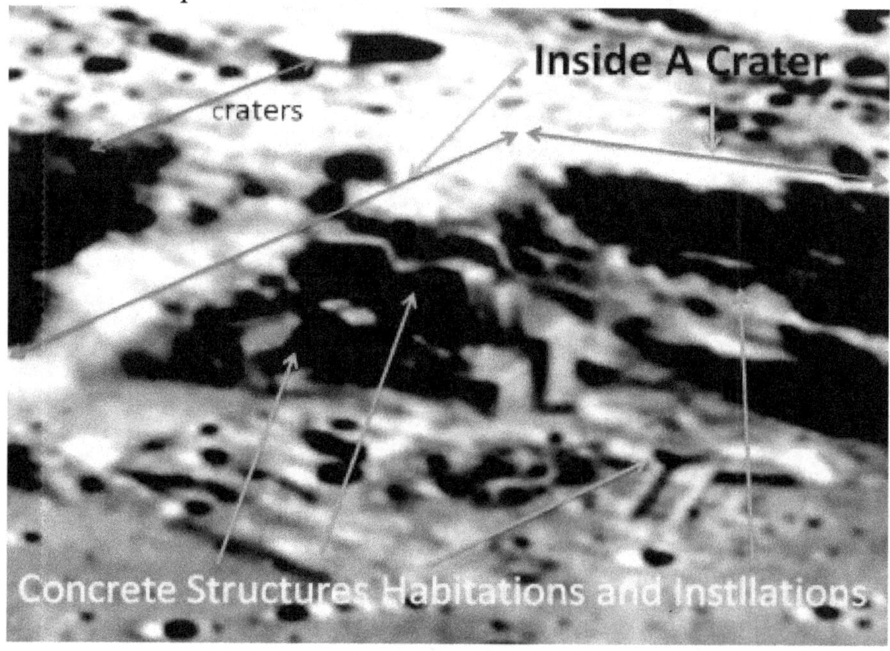

Others great Towns layouts like the plans for earth towns The immense size is clear when compare it to the neighbor crater

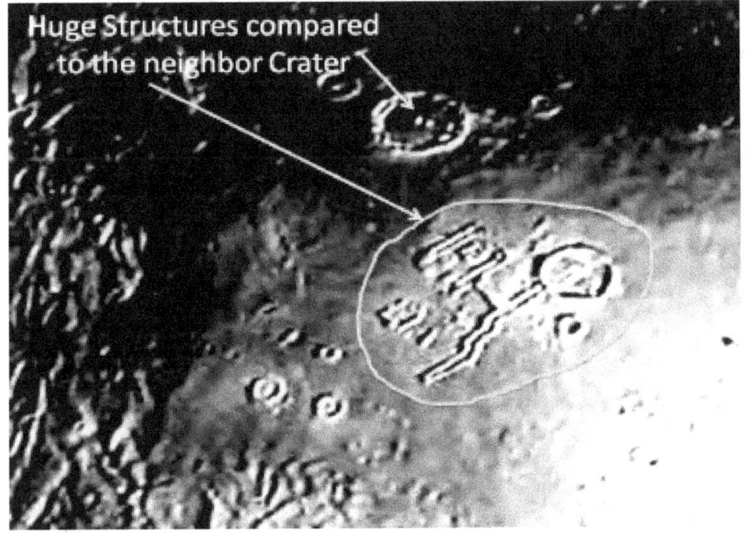

Another immense structures mostly huge factories:

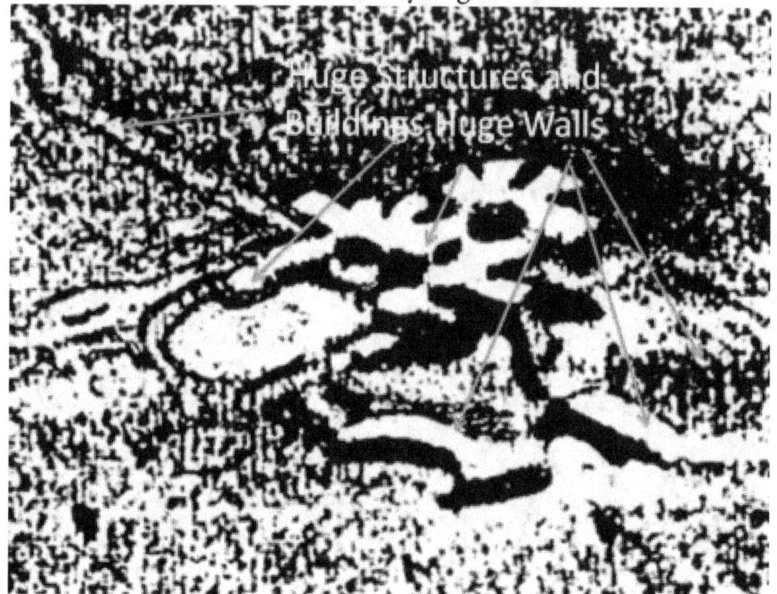

Other discoveries on the moon, is the presence of mini spacecraft that's accompanied the astronauts from time to time in their walks, also kinds of sensors connected to the land of the moon that light and send visual signals of light when astronaut approaches them, it is clear that they are security sensors alerting the presence of a stranger in these areas and borders .This image taken from a NASA video showing the astronaut dancing with the sensors when he approaches, the sensor flashing with light, when he goes way, the sensor light disappears.

A "Crystal Palace" or a glass palace, with a form of inverted great radar or a Dome like in the South Pole human stations, beside it there are others great structures with houses:

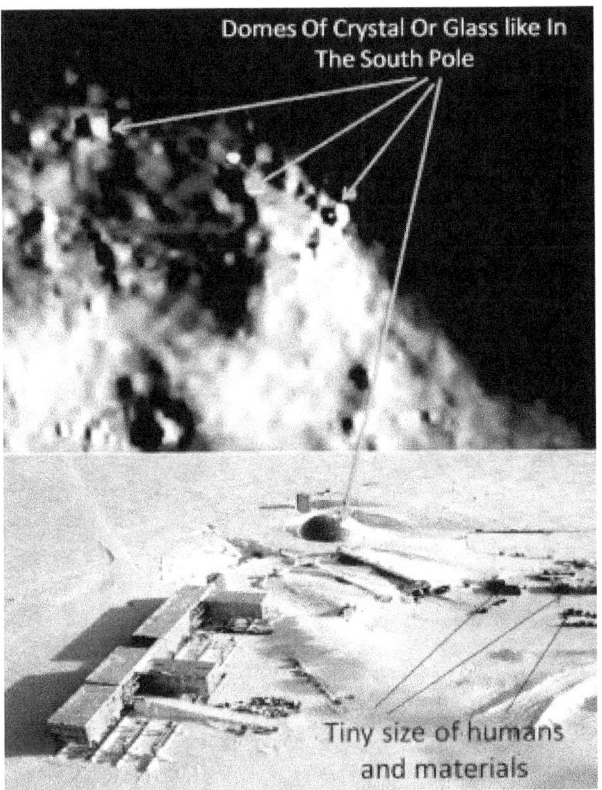
Domes Of Crystal Or Glass like In
The South Pole
Tiny size of humans
and materials

Another huge construction of walls like the great wall of china, also contains houses:

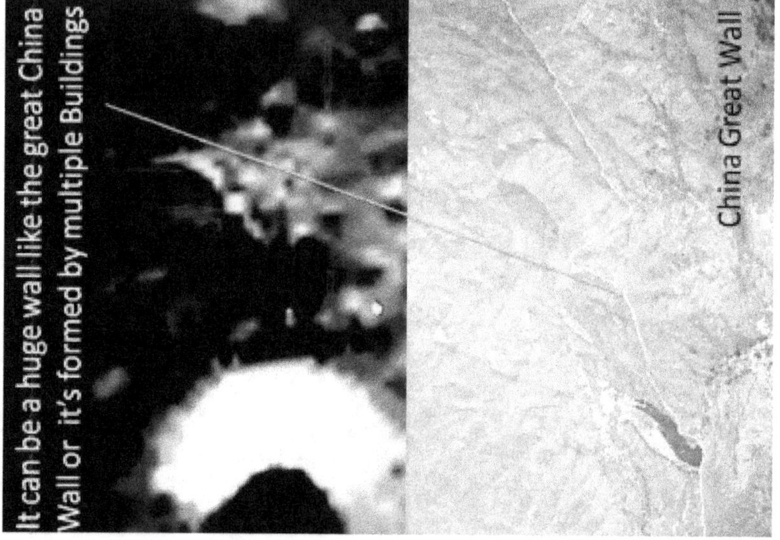

This photos shows a Nazis base in Schrödinger Crater photographed by the Cassiopeia Probe .The diameter of the Crater is 1.5 Km (4921 Feet).

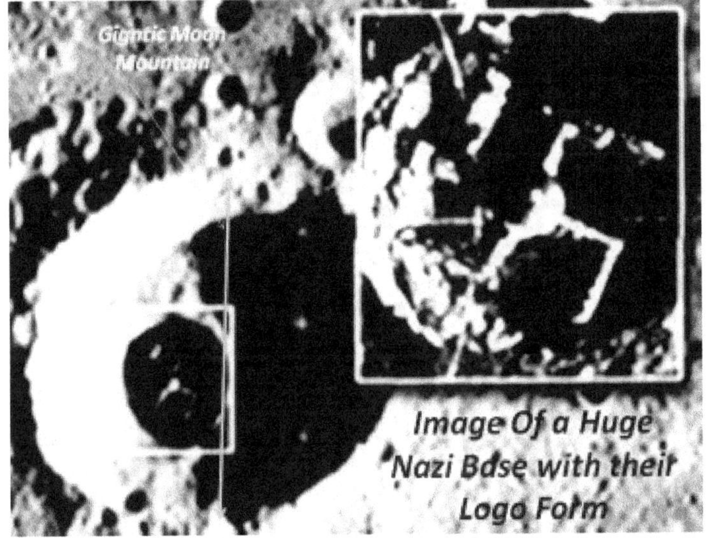

Photos from the moon presenting a Haunebu machines:

C.8: The Los Angeles Raid In 1942

The Spot Light Converged On a Huge Body Which is A Nazi UFO

In The 25th of February 1942, a raid from Nazis UFOs occurred over Los Angeles. Air raid sirens sounded and it was received by 1400 anti-aircraft shells, the anti-aircraft guns were unstoppable and blazing but the UFOs were invincible and untouchable with the 12.8 pounds ammunitions. This was very strange at that time as they thought they were Japanese planes.

The UFOs filmed at that time were in the form of light balls appearing and disappearing in the sky.

The military huge light spots converged in a body of a huge UFO meanwhile the other balls of light continues to appears and disappears without being hitted by the artillery arms.

The itinerary of the Nazi UFO started from the Pacific Ocean to Santa Monica then long beach and Huntington Beach. He returned via the same itinerary and disappeared in the ocean from the radar systems. The fires were opened in Los Angeles the spotlights or the search light in the same location.

Itinerary Followed By The Nazi UFO

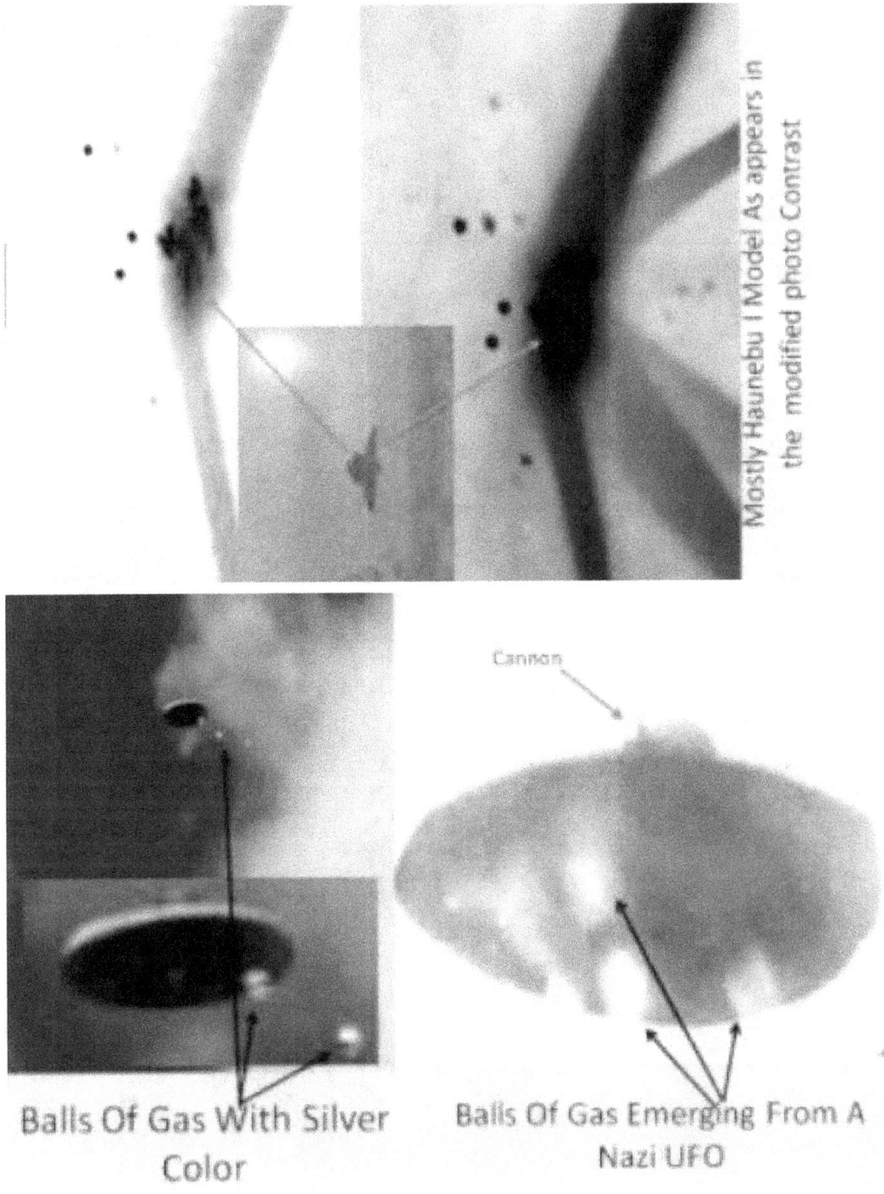

The central UFO photographed was in the form of a Haunebu I Nazi model that supports 8 humans as crew and has a diameter of 25 meters with a minimum speed of 4700 km per hour. The balls of lights can be just a spherical forms made by the Nazi crew or a small flying saucers made too by Nazis especially we see nowadays these balls appears and disappears quickly in the modern UFOs sightings.

The UFO comes from Santa Monica with a speed of 25 miles in 30 minutes which is a very low speed. This make me thinking that it was a cooperative conspiracy between some hidden parts in both sides especially when we know that one day before a Japanese submarine fired 25 shells into an oil field in Goleta near Santa Barbara.

As Nazis gave Mitsubishi at that time motors for flying saucers opens new theories about the Japanese owning of UFOs from that era until today.

Five Americans died as a consequence of this night some from heart attacks others from the exploded debris ammunitions falling on them. Properties Damages were recorded too for the same cause.

The press wrote a lot about this incident some claimed that they were just baloons other said that it was fake alarm nothing in the sky.

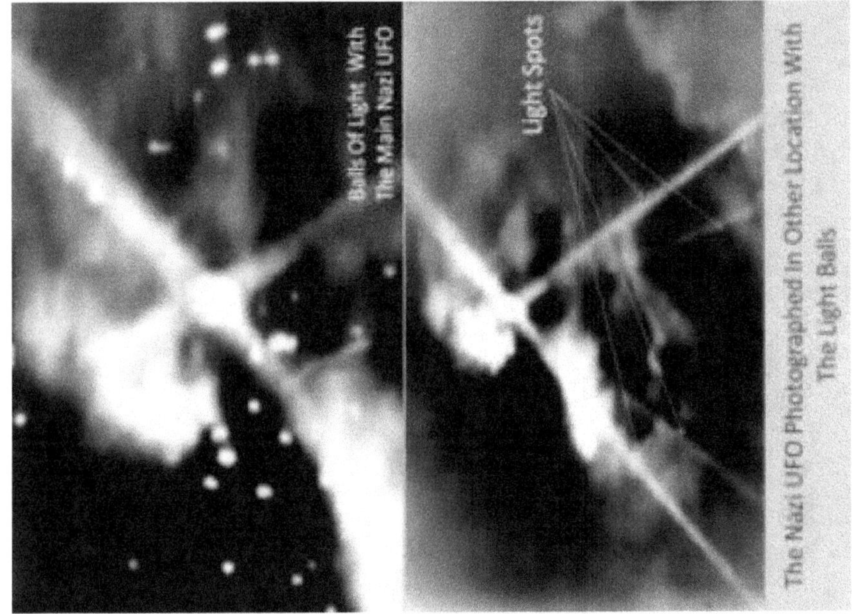
Balls Of Light With
The Main Nazi UFO
Light Spots
The Nazi UFO Photographed In Other Location With
The Light Balls

Searchlights and Anti-aircraft Guns Comb Sky
WAR EXTRA
Los Angeles Examiner
AIR BATTLE RAGES OVER LOS ANGELES
The Greater Herald Examiner
DID US MILITARY ATTACK A UFO IN 1942 OVER LA?
ARMY SAYS ALARM REAL
Examples Of Press Coverage For The Incident
ANTI-AIRCRAFT GUNS BLAST AT L. A. MYSTERY INVADER
News-Press
Raid Scare Blacks Out Southland, but Knox Claims False Alarm
Press-Telegram
GUNS BOMBARD SKY AS STRANGE PLANE
BLACK OUT SOUTHLAND IN FIRST RAID
WILMIN
Stimson Says Enemy Agents Operated Planes
Flight Over L. A. Harbor District Yesterday
Allies Giving Nippons Hard Pounding
Los Angeles Times
9 A.M. FINAL
MYSTERY AIR OBJECTS SEEN IN SKY OVER L.A.
Los Angeles Times
ARMY SAYS ALARM REAL

C.9: Why Nazis UFOs didn't overcome USA Until Today?

In The World War II

The sightings of Nazi's UFOs was earlier than the world war 2.The SS: *Schutzstaffel(protection body)* was the pioneer of the program of the development of the Nazi's flying saucers program as its logo is marked on so many of them .The Nazi's flying saucers were unable to carry huge bombs and throw on cities like Washington D.C in USA or London in UK or any other capital worldwide .All the Nazi's UFOs has gun machines and canon and some are designed to transport troops of soldiers and militaries. So, primarily it's a technical problem with the designs.

After The World War II Until Today

This is the big question: if the Nazis are really alive up today what are they waiting for to revenge from the USA as she was the key factor for the loose of the third Reich in the war? Then coming UK, France, USSR or today Russia and other countries ?

The USA led Expeditions from 1928 via Richard Byrd multiple missions to others like Lincoln Ellsworth, Finn Ronne to the fifties and sixties operations like Windmill and Deep Freeze .In the years 1957-1958, assisted The International Geophysical Year that was the final step to the Atlantic Treaty between the 12 involved countries which has earlier Antarctica discoveries like Belgium, Germany, UK, France, Chile, Brazil, etc.

This Treaty increased in countries number to 29 then to 54.The main agreement was and still on: Forbidding the military existence on Antarctica and limit it to the scientific research teams and civilians.

When we return to the big incident occurred in 1947 for the American Expedition to Antarctica led by The Admiral Richard Evelyn Byrd when the Nazi's UFOs emerged from the Atlantic Ocean and clashed with the ships with phenomenal uncaught speed, we should ask a question: does this incident beside the several sightings in world war 2 by the allies pilots, the Nazi's UFOs prototypes and documents found in Germany by the allies, the sightings over USA of Nazi's UFOs, the famous Roswell incident in 1947, pushed the American Officials to be a peaceful mediator between countries clashes like between Chile, UK, France and Brazil to attain and sign the Atlantic Treaty?

All this to avoid a conflict with the Nazis at that time despite we know that USA has atomic bombs which can be used against them in Antarctica and destroys their bases in silence .Does the US officials were astonished and overwhelmed by the Nazis technology of flying saucers and preferred waiting until they developed their own flying saucers then they enter in fight with them ?But a new question emerges here, for over a 70 years now, what they are waiting for to fight the Nazis or there's another explanation ignored by the majority of the world which will be the biggest surprise?

What I remarked too from the different Expeditions sent by different countries worldwide is that firstly, the expeditions placed are fixed sites that's means they can't move for long distances for new unvisited or undiscovered locations; secondly most of the expeditions located near the Nazi's discovered land in the world war 2 in north Antarctica in the area known as Queen Maud Land, are closed after a period, we have examples like India, USA, Norway, Sweden, United Kingdom and Soviet Union.

Mostly it was concluded a secret agreement between the SS (The Schutzstaffel) Nazi leaders or generals responsible for the UFOs and Andromeda Programs and some USA military Officials .I think the common factor shared between those Nazis and the US military Officials that they were high ranking freemasonry grades!

This is the only logical and credible explanation for me about the question asking why the Nazis UFOs didn't destroy USA in WWII ?

They leave time to the Americans to develop their own flying saucers in area 51 and S4 and so many secret bases because both Sides works for only target which is preparing the necessary flying saucers numbers to make in a due day a fake aliens invasion on the entire earth .Why this fake aliens invasion? It's to kill 7 billions of humans and concentrating 500 millions on Greater Israel Kingdom between Euphrates river in Iraq and Nile River in Egypt .

How is that can be real? Simply for two causes: The first one is the world war one and the world war two and the Zionism creation all of them created by the 33 degree Free masons.

How did I knew it? From the leaked letter found in the pocket of a messenger hitted by a thunderstorm lightning in 1871.This letter was sent from Albert Pike who was a Jew as his mother was a Jew, to someone named "Morino" (it's important for me to mention here that there's not any kind of implicit or explicit hatred inciting against The Jews and Judaism religion; criminals and bad people exists in Islam in Christianity in Hinduism in Buddhism in Atheism, this is a common factor in humans) .Albert Pike was a general in the American army in the civil war and it was judged by treason but as he has 33 degree free masonry degree he was granted an amnesty.

This letter talked about The first and second world wars planning and the political movement named "Zionism" that was not yet created, the first conference of the Zionism was in 1897 in Basel Switzerland that's means 26 years after the leak of this letter, that's confirms that the 33 degree free masons created this political movement from the Nothing sponsored it with money and press marketing for their proper agenda, the secret target.

The apparent part of this target is clear : Greater Israel Kingdom between rivers Euphrates of Iraq and Nile of Egypt for Zionists-Jews but the secret target is this kingdom is not for Jews, it will be for the Satan Worshipping himself and personally the Satan who gave the apple for our father Adam and mother Eve in the paradise .They simply apply the plan transferred from generation to other through the centuries from about 6000 years ago when Bakhtansar the Babylon King came to Palestine and took all the Jews(most of them were Children Of Israel) there to Babylon for forty years .

The 33 degree free masons call this event as: The First Rupture which means the first rupture from Palestine land and the highest ranking free masons(30-31-32) knows this despite they're not Jews. Some of The Infidel Rabbis wrote the Talmud of Babylon which is not the Jews holy book(Torah is the only Jews holy Book) and its main idea was the creation of Greater

Israel Kingdom to defeat God Faith on earth and challenge God himself on earth.

This kingdom should sizes 500 million humans not more, this number is the accepted level for them called " The Quorum", they can guarantee the eat and drink for them and especially the continuous surveillance day and night as Greater Israel will be a great dictatorship not a democracy. To attains this Quorum, they need to kill 7 billions of humans .How will they do this?

With the "Fake Aliens Invasion" and this is the secret Tie between the SS generals and the US Officials belonging to Free masonry and this is the real cause behind the question why The Nazis didn't attacked USA until today and vice versa .

The Nazis with their sophisticated developed technology's UFOs for 80 years now beside the American, France, UK, Canadians, Russians, Chinese will participates in a fake aliens invasion that they prepare us for it now for decades via their mystery documentaries, their Hollywood movies ,their television series, their kid's cartoons, their daily news sightings and now via internet with the normal people recording worldwide with their smart phones and everyone is happy when he catch a UFO with his camera.

The fake aliens invasion was mentioned the first time by the Nazi engineer the pioneer of the American Space program after the world war 2: Wernher Von Braun.

When he was in his death bed, he said to Doctor Carol Rosin that there are some people preparing for a fake aliens invasion. He mentioned this after steps taken from the US Elites as excuses to weaponize the space: the first one is Russians or Soviets at that time as an enemy (here you should remark that conflicts were and are artificial not natural as they appears they are created by the Freemasonry but none can see that as they are propagated worldwide in different countries for centuries now).

The second excuse is the terrorism and you have now great info about terrorism and who are they .The third excuse is the "Third World countries crisis" and sure you listen about South America, South East Asia and Africa problems especially the floods of illegal immigrants.

The fourth excuse is "The asteroids" based on my research I can confirm to you that they prepares unfortunately for an asteroids and meteors showers to kill maximum of lives and to make humanity more tired and exhausted beside Wars, the economic crisis, climate change crisis, pandemic crisis like the Covid-19 created by them in "Institut Pasteur" in France in 2004 with a patent and sent to China but mainstream media don't talk about that as they own them.

This exhausting facilitates the acceptance of the fake aliens invasion which is the fifth excuse to weaponize the space as Von Braun thought but for me all is for Greater Israel Kingdom.

In the nineties of the twentieth century a Canadian Journalist known as Serge Monast talked about secret project called Blue Beam Project prepared by NASA and United Nations to make a fake aliens invasion .

Both of the two men didn't knew who is really behind this crime against humanity but me finally I knew who are they really and have the proofs which I'll show for you on this chapter.

Before that, you should know that there's 4.7 millions Freemasons Worldwide infiltrated for centuries now not decades generations after generations in very sensitive posts including : Parliaments, ministers of defense and interiors, Presidents, Politicians, Business men, Singers, Actors, TV Presenters, etc .Most of Freemasonry followers don't know anything about this project or other ones working in parallel .

The middle ranking Freemasons like the 17th degree and higher acquires the feeling that they were manipulated and oriented to the Satan worshipping some of them leaves, others continues .They request from them immolation or sacrifices by slaughtering kids as innocent Souls to the Satan!

A French Christian former Freemason with 16th Degree, Maurice Caillet said : "I prefer to stay poor and believer rather than rich and Satan Worshipper"!

The Freemasonry has approximately five centuries as age founded in Russia, it was and it's a continuation for "The Illuminatis" who were their ancestors in the medieval ages Their existence became felt in the 17th century when the Rothschild family found the banking system in Europe, 99% of banks are under their control and when we say banks that's means all the monetary flows including Stocks.

In 1917 they gave a loan to UK with a 2000 million dollars, in compensation: make Palestine as a Patron or Homeland for The Jews! This loan was a need for UK in the World War One and Palestine was under its occupation, this agreement is known under the name of: Balfour Declaration or Promise .This agreement was between Lord Arthur Balfour the Secretary Of State For Foreign Affairs of Great Britain Empire and Lord Walter Rothschild both of them were members of the Conservative Political Party.

Now I want from you to link these points: from the sixteen century the creation of Freemasonry to the foundation of banking system then the creation of Zionism in 1871 by the 33 degree free mason Albert Pike then the Belfour Declaration or promise by The Rothschild's then the fake aliens invasion .Did you notice that this is not a conspiracy theory and it's a real conspiracy?

Serge Monast talked about four major steps that will be applied by United Nations and NASA that are for me just tools in the hands of the 33 degree Freemasons.

The United Nations founded in 1918 by The Rothschild's and The Rockfeller's its name was: The League Of Nations and recognized the Belfour Declaration in 1922 as a legitimized legal treaty and you can verify by yourself!

You can see now nothing is in coincidence .NASA created in 1958 to manipulate all the so called modern sciences or the Free masonry science in majority with my point of view (remark here that this was at least 12 years after the obligatory recruitment of 1600 Nazis staff in different military and science fields including Wernher Von Braun).

The four major steps are : Step 1: The Break Down of All Archaeological Knowledge ,Step 2: The Massive Space Show in the Sky, Step 3: Two Way Electronic Thought Control ,Step 4: Supernatural Manifestations Using Secret Technology

My point of view is that those steps are in reality four great projects occurring in parallel after the world War 2 until the day of the great show in the sky or the massive space show worldwide which is here the step 2.All the other steps are used to serve the step 2 which is for me the final step.

The supernatural manifestations using secret technology is proved by different holograms or 3D projections in the sky and in the ground presenting sacred symbols for all the religions, heavens ones: Judaism,

Christianity and Islam and man-made ones: Hinduism, Buddhism, Sikhism and others.

Those holograms are two types: statics without movement and dynamics with movement. The main target of these holograms is making people WorldWide feeling that they are in the right path as God specify them with their own religion's holy symbols .Every religion followers feels that they are the chosen ones.

The step 3, the two way electronic communication thought control is working with and for the step 2: religion followers thinks that God communicate with them and they communicate with him The communication is telepathic and spiritual. It's too via the electronic devices and internet.

For the Christians and Christianity as it's the first heaven religion in number of followers on earth, they sent and still sending Mary the Virgin dynamic hologram in different places Worldwide. For example this image is from a video amateur recording this event in South Africa and naturally the crowd reaction is this is a message from God and we are in the right path.

Mostly this video was recorded in 2008 but some returns it to Mai 21st 2013.

Dynamic Hologram Of Mary The Virgin In
The Sky.Huge light In Background & Thick
Form of The Hologram
Forest Trees
Forest Trees

Mary the Virgin Static Hologram appeared in Italy in March 27, 2020, this is the Picture:

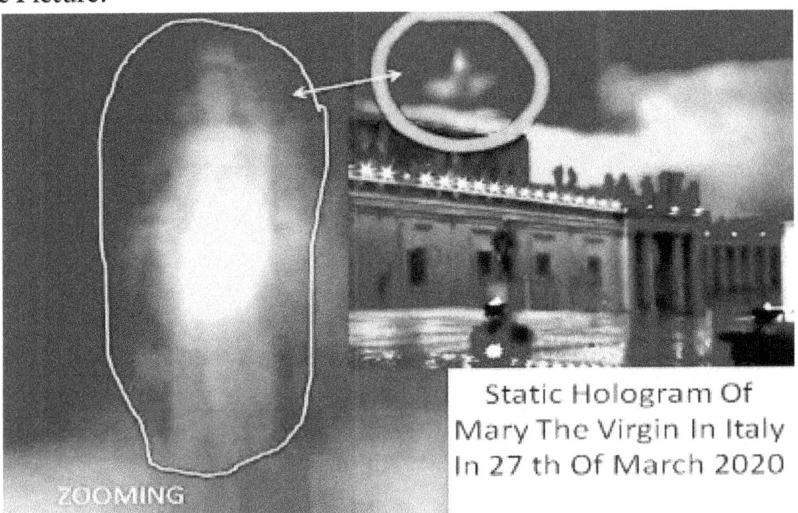

In Colombia, the 27th of March 2020, this static Hologram of Mary the Virgin appeared too:

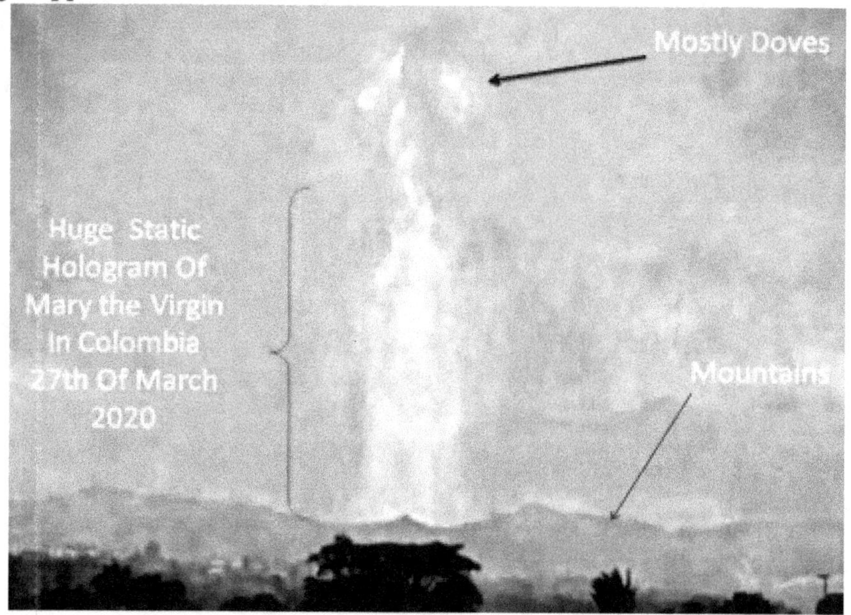

These are some static holograms for Mary the Virgin from the entire world in unknown locations for me until the writing of this book:

Static Hologram Of Mary Holding
Jesus and Seeing The Sky Light

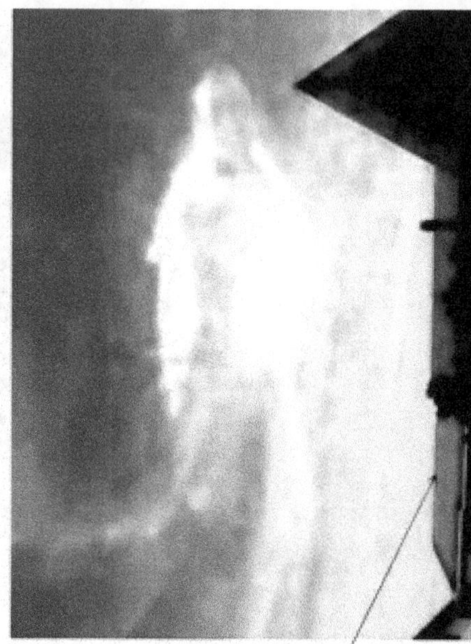

Static Hologram Of Mary The Virgin In
Horizontal Direction.The Image is With 90 °

Multiple Static Holograms Of
Mary With multiple Locations

A dynamic Hologram appeared in South America with movements up and down , left and right and especially flashing light as the Hologram communicate with the crowds .The images below are from the same moment's video but the second appears as it's in the dark cause of caption the image from a video record:

The Second State A Ball Of Light
For The Flashing Of The Hologram

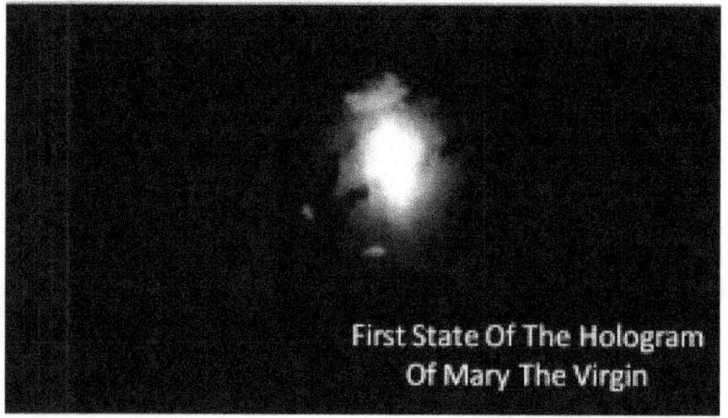

Mary the Virgin dynamic holograms appeared in Egypt in multiple locations and in a separated periods. The last appearance as I know is in Alwarraq in Giza in a Friday of December 11th 2009 between 1 AM to 4 AM, known as "Our Lady Of Warraq" .

This apparition occurred in the church of Coptic Orthodox Mary The Virgin and Archangel Michael, it was reported by a Muslim neighbor while he was sitting in his Coffee Shop. The hologram was moving from the central dome to twin domes.

This event recorded with people's smart phones and reported locally and in the international press like Los Angeles Times, Agence France Press (AFP), Italian Asia News and British Middle East Online .It's also recurred several times in the same year.

The dynamic hologram moves over the Front door between the twin domes:

Hologram Of
Mary The
Virgin
Cross Of
The
Church
Approx.The
Same Photo
but from an
Egyptian
Coptic
Television

The dynamic hologram of Mary the Virgin is over the principal dome of the Church moving between it and the smaller ones:

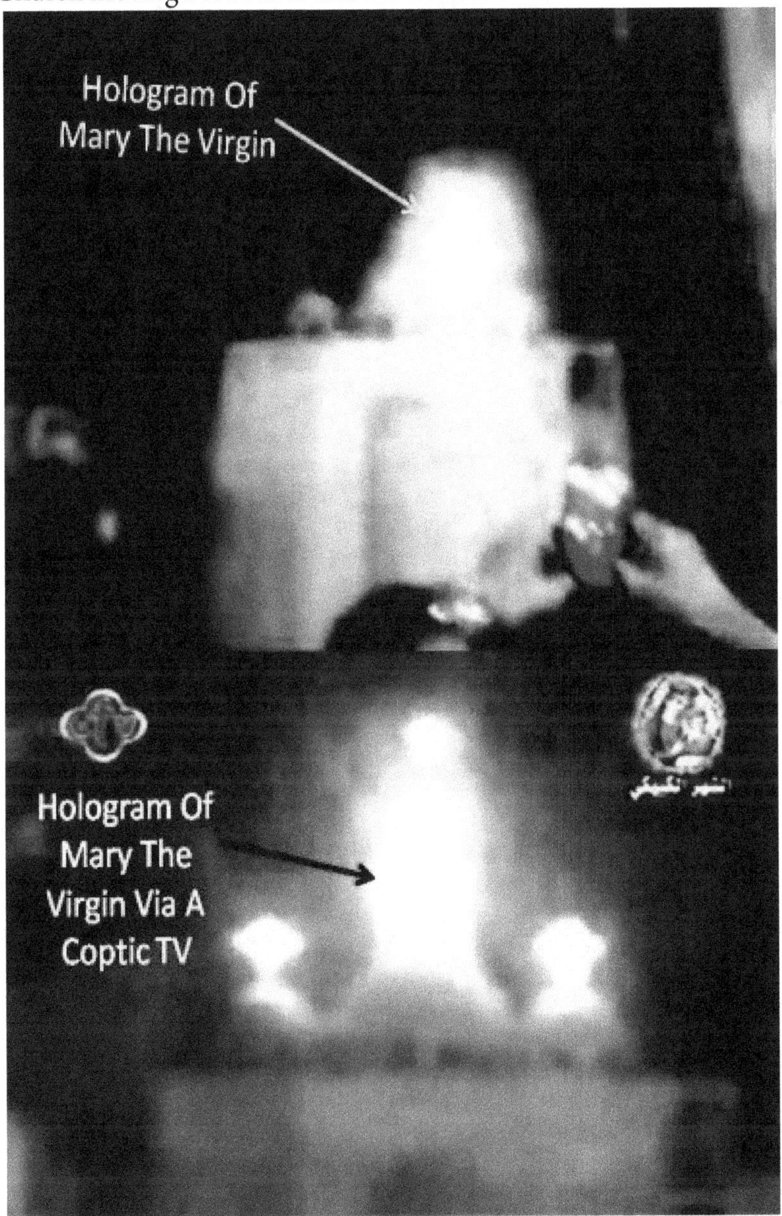

An Orange colored ball flying over the main or principle dome building over the three crosses filmed by Christians Smart Phone:

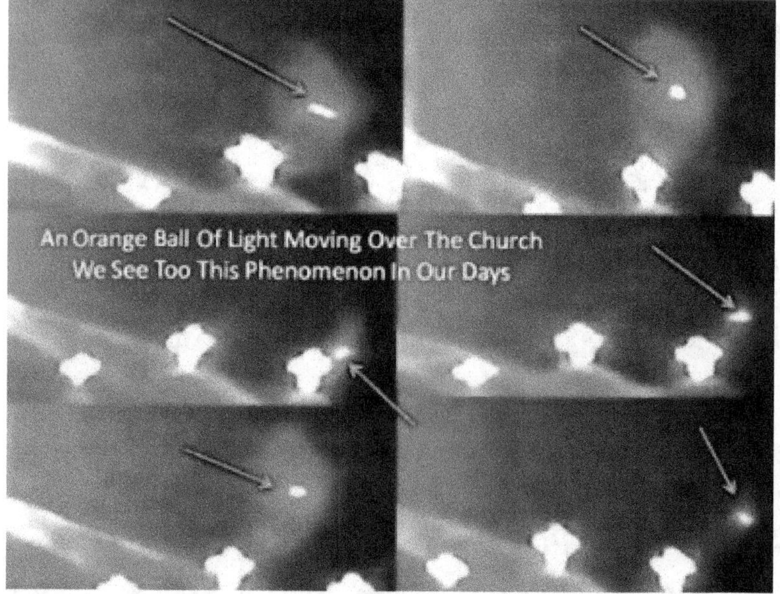

A blue colored sphere displaced in the sky irregularly accompanied the apparition of the hologram:

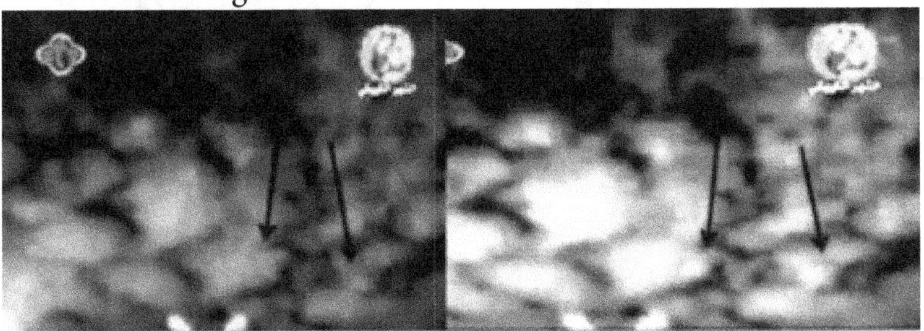

Presence of Christians and Muslims crowds recorded:

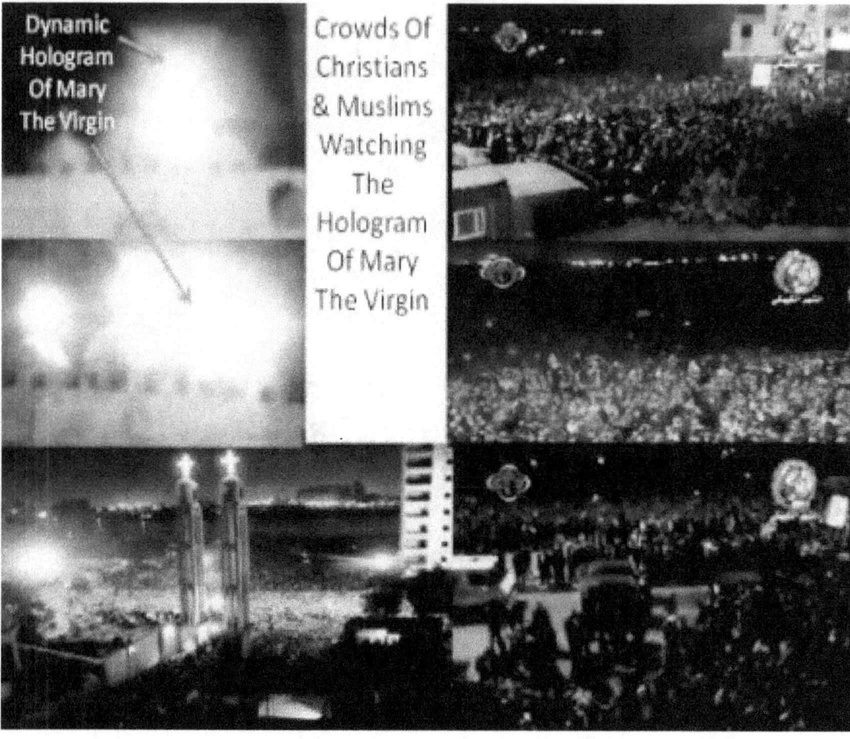

Between the years 2000 and 2001, the Mary Virgin's hologram appeared in Assiut above the dome of Saint Mark's Church known as "Our Lady Of Assiut".

The Virgin appeared surrounded with pigeons or doves above her .Mostly the contour is with lights with pigeon forms. The international press talked about this event like BBC and AFP beside the national media like Watani Newspaper.

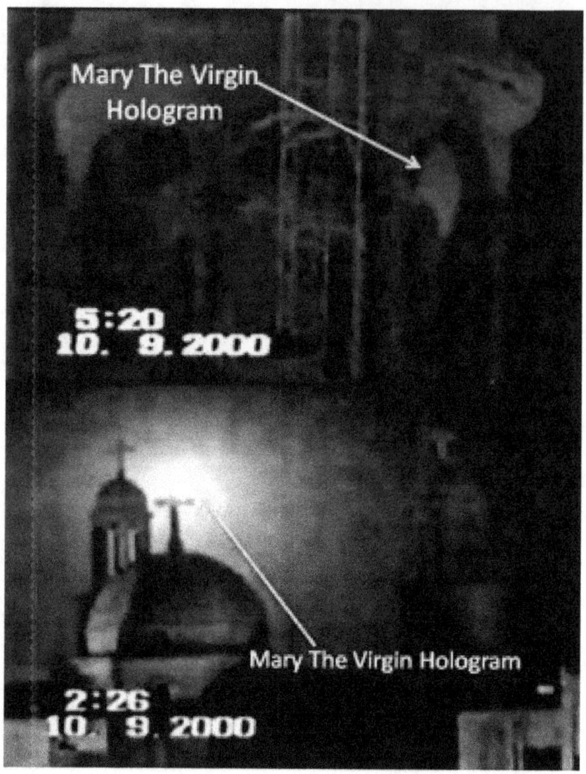
Mary The Virgin
Hologram
5:20
10. 9. 2000
Mary The Virgin Hologram
2:26
10. 9. 2000

Some apparitions were in the form of doves:

Another famous apparition of the dynamic hologram of Mary the virgin was known as "The Lady Of Zeitoun", it was in 1968 when two Muslim neighbors worked as bus mechanics saw a lady from above the Saint Mary Coptic Church attempting to commit suicide they called the police

They discovered later that it was a light form moving between domes' church and it became known as the lady Mary. The sightings were frequent between 1968 to 1971, three years of consecutive apparitions of this hologram. The event was widely covered by media inside and outside of Egypt even Jamal AbdelNasser The Former Egyptian President recognized it, tens of thousands saw this event.

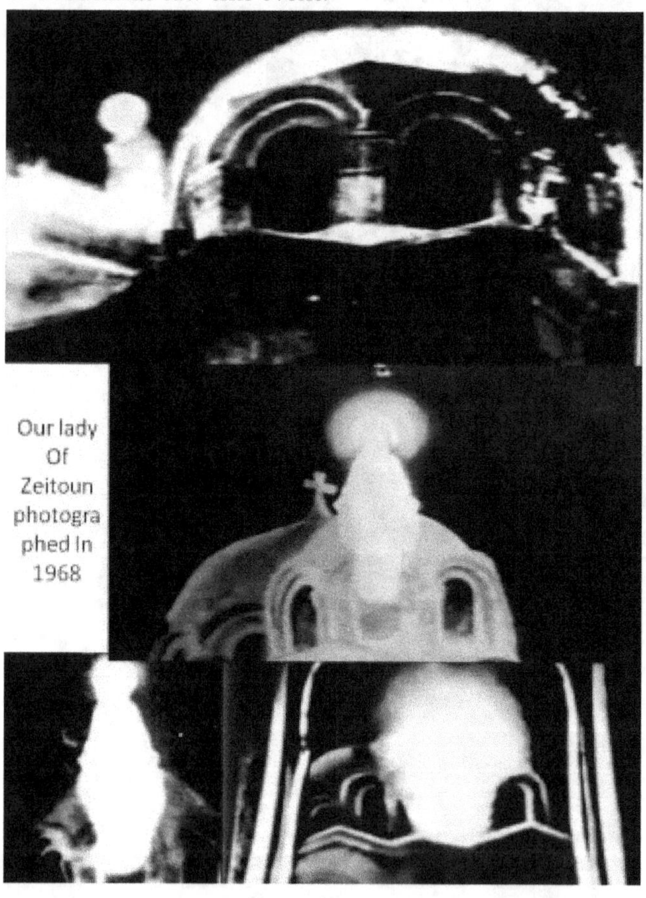

The lightening doves accompanied the apparition:

Examples of articles talking about the apparition in AlZeitoun in 1969:

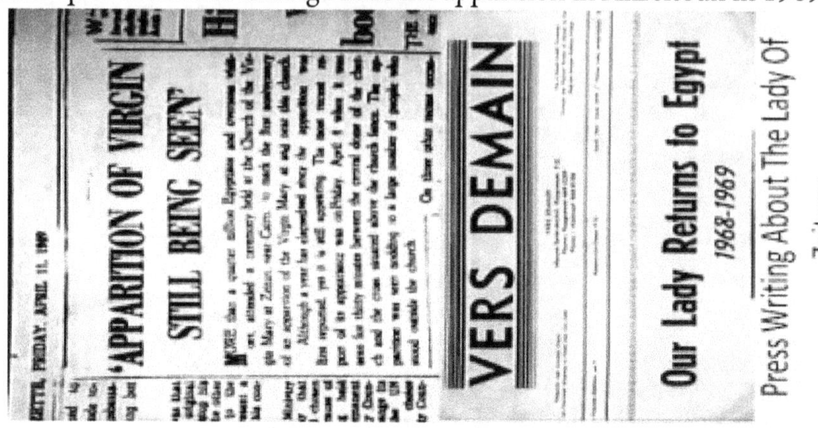

Press Writing About The Lady Of Zeitoun

Crowds of Christians and Muslims were always following the apparitions:

In a famous town called " Harissa" in Lebanon, a static hologram of Mary The Virgin appeared for several times near the statue of Mary a touristic pole:

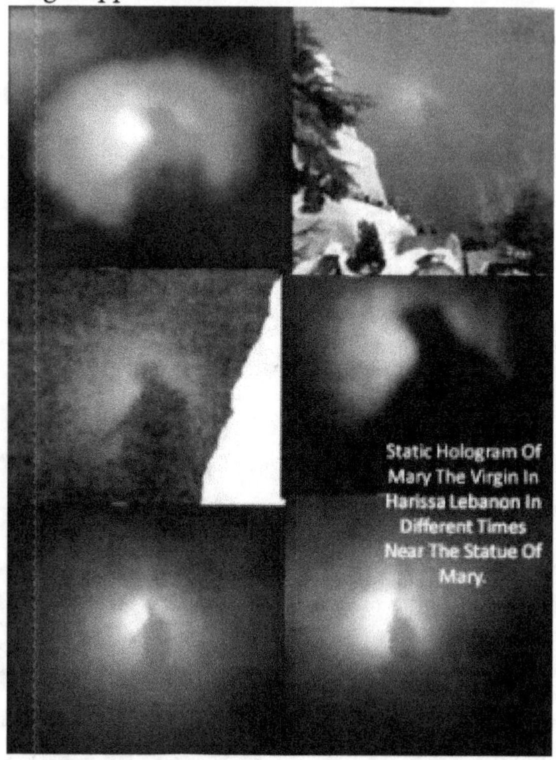

Did you notice that Egypt embraced so many holograms apparition of Mary The Virgin? Did you notice too that the technology of holography or 3D projection in the air with the complete control of movement is already existed from at least 1968? Meanwhile the 3D concept and technology appeared in the so called fourth industrial and scientific evolution with the movie "Avatars" for James Cameroun and the 3D printing technology!

Did you smell here something not good? I give you the answer: this technology and so many others are already developed from the twentieth century based on two arguments, the first one is the science of the savant Nikola Tesla and so many scientists at that time and the second argument is the technology transferred by the Aliens the runners of the UFO after the Agreement between USA and the Greys in 1956 in Florida, they give them the permission to abduct and kidnapping any human in counterpart their knowledge and science.

The 33 degree Freemasons the real governors of the world oriented the humanity to a specified direction in technology and science especially the propulsion system in rockets from the Nazis based on combustion meanwhile the high developed science and technology like the UFOs and Laser as examples are staying for them and in their agenda service like the fake aliens invasion one and other fields like the climate manipulation.

Today we have NASA, Virgin Galactic, Blue Origin and Space X as the pioneers of the space technology meanwhile the UFO technology is already here for 80 years developed by Nazis, Americans, Russians, the British, Canadians and even Brazilians to the due date of the fake Aliens invasion.

Why the multiple sightings of Mary the Virgin in Egypt from an early date? Simply, based on the 33 degree Freemasons, Egypt will be the capital of Greater Israel Kingdom as Children Of Israel were enslaved by the Moses' Pharaoh and it's the first border of this Kingdom, the second one is Iraq.

It's not yet secret the Greater Israel Project as the politicians like : Benjamin Netanyahu, Naftali Bennett the new Israeli prime minister, David Ben Gurion, Moshe Dayan, Menachem Begin and others talked and talks publicly about Greater Israel project without any shame or fear despite they're manipulated too by the 33 Degree Freemasons who convinced them indirectly that it will be for Jews but it's not true it will be for the Satan

Worshipping to defeat God faith on earth and Judaism is a heaven religion of faith in God and never it was or will be a Satan worshipping religion.

As I said the holography existed for long time another proof for this, is the Japanese Cartoon series from 1978: "Conan, The Future Boy Or Future Boy Conan" when Lana, her friends and her grandfather in the central tower showing her a virtual reality of sky, sun, people, baby playing with ball, trees, voices, etc but she's involved in this system completely until she cried from fear when she thought she holds a baby and he surpassed her. This kind of cartoons is for the subliminal message programming people to accept the future events with their subconscious.

The Grand Father push a button a holy Garden with people, vegetation and animals created when Lana tried to hold a baby he surpassed her she was shocked

Jesus Christ Static Hologram appeared in several countries and with several forms.

These images series are from a south east Asia country mostly The Philippines based on people photographed in the footage:

A ball of light in the clouds moves from left to right to uncover the face of Jesus-Christ:

It's For Jesus-Christ   The hair is clear over the Head-Skull.
Ball Of Light moves From Left To Right Then appears the Skull-Face

Static Hologram Of Jesus Christ In Horizontal
Position as In The Bed

In Lebanon a dynamic Hologram of Jesus Christ recorded emerging from the sea to the sky through a hole of light .The Lebanese crowd crying(Ya Allah...Oh God) from the joy:

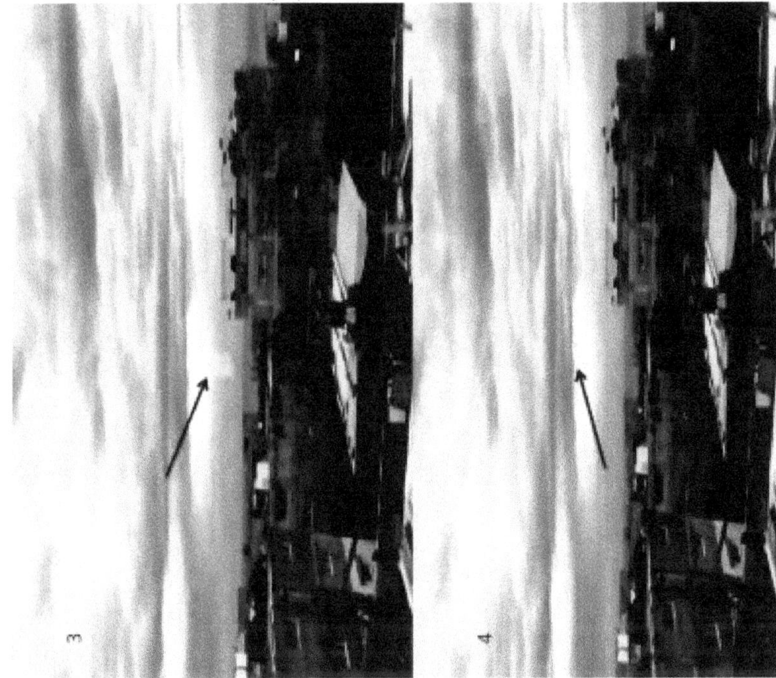

Dynamic Hologram Of Jesus Christ Enter To The Light's Hole In The Sky

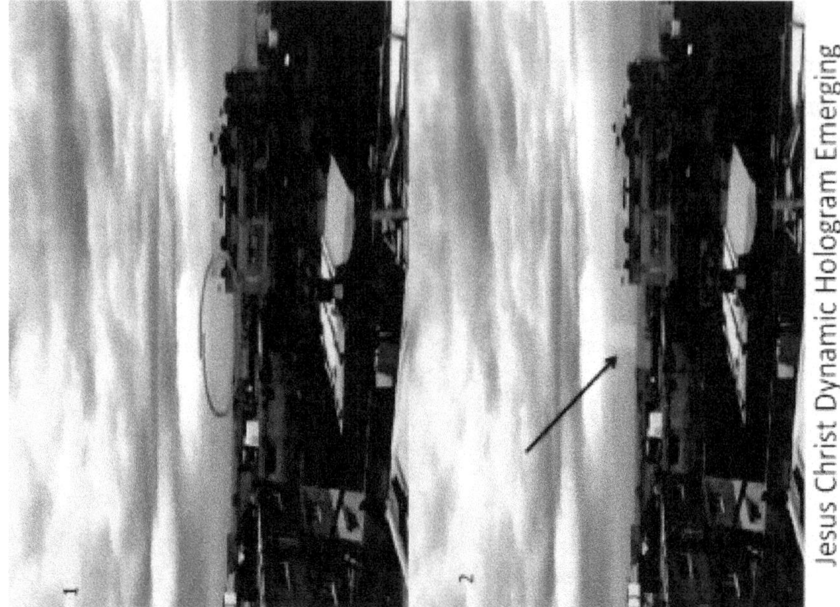

Jesus Christ Dynamic Hologram Emerging From Sea To The Sky Through A Light Hole

In Calsas Colombia and in Argentina Static holograms appeared:

The Cross and the Crucified Jesus Christ appeared in several countries worldwide:

The Cross & The
Crucified Jesus
Christ Worldwide

A Static Hologram in the form of an Angel appeared in the sky of South Carolina in USA, it was recorded by a man called Corey Heron who thought that this is his protecting Angel as he said to really his speech to Inside Edition program:

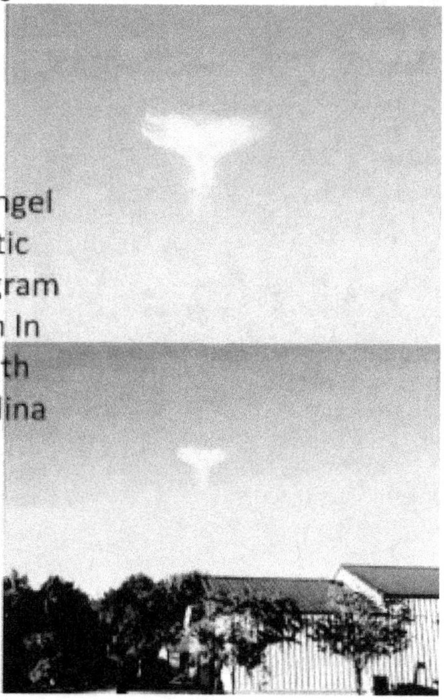

An Angel Static Hologram Seen In South Carolina

So many Angels Static Holograms were seen Worldwide:

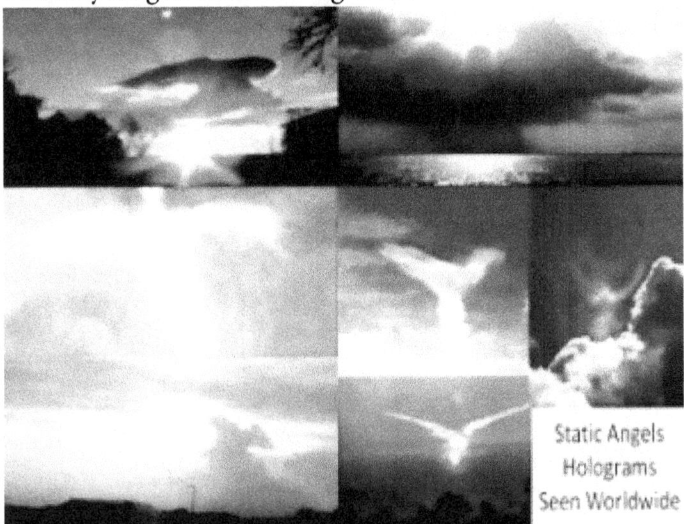

For The Jews and Christians in the same time they sent and still sending The Lion Of Judah. The Lion Of Judah is a symbol for the tribe of Judah one of Jacob twelve sons. It's sacred in Judaism and Christian theology. It's a sign for them for the second coming of Jesus Christ.

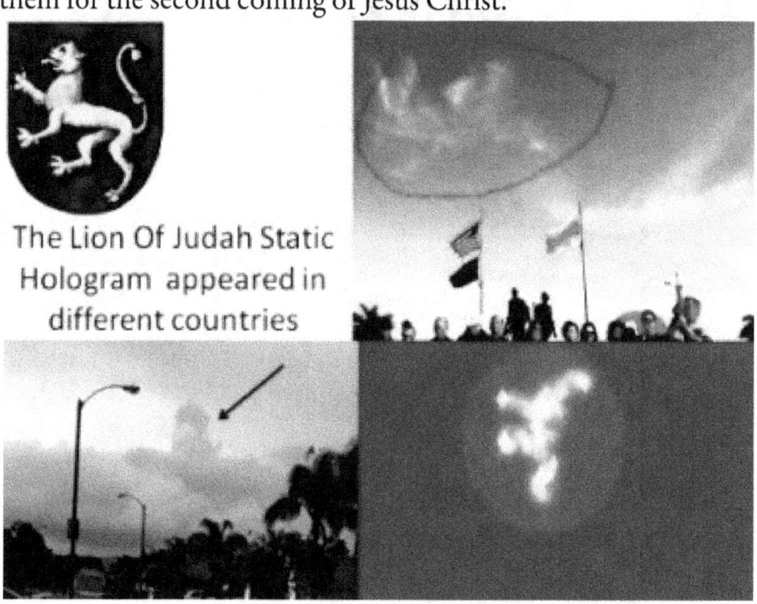

The Lion Of Judah Static Hologram appeared in different countries

For the new Jewish year, the 33 degree Freemasons sent a dynamic-static hologram in the form of the iris and pupil of an eye over Jerusalem accompanied with a trumpet sounds from the sky. The message is: The eye of the freemasonry is on Jerusalem you are under our control. It's not a message of love simply because Jerusalem is the hub and the symbol of the three heaven religions: Judaism, Christianity and Islam, Freemasonry aims to transform these faith religions and other ones like Buddhism and Hinduism on earth to one world religion which is: The Satan Worshipping. The static-dynamic hologram:

The Iris Of The Freemasonry Eye From
Another Angle

The Clouds are moving on the circle
borders

Under the step 4 of Blue Beam Project: The supernatural manifestations using secret technology. On Ground, they sent Dynamic Holograms for Mary the Virgin in several churches:

Dynamic Holograms Of Mary The Virgin In Some Churches Worldwide

On the ground too, they sent dynamic holograms for Jesus Christ in so many fields from rivers to forests to statues:

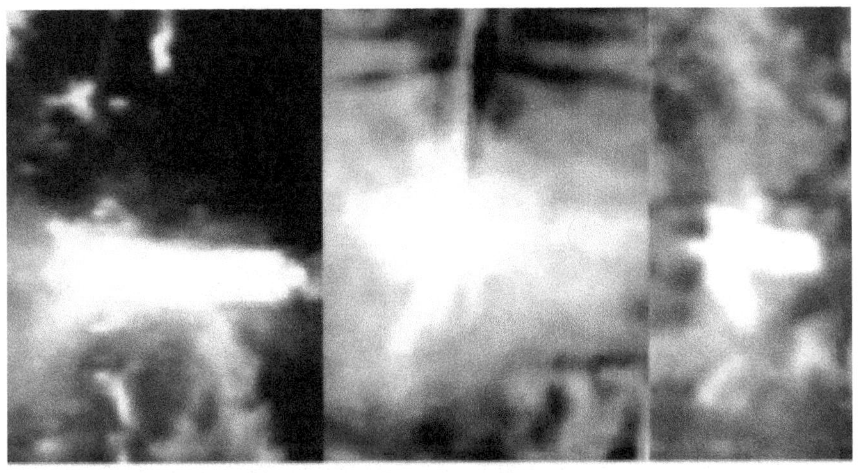

Dynamic Holograms For Jesus Christ Over The surface of Rivers in Three Different Locations

7
8
7
9
4
5
6
1
2
3
Steps
From The
Ground
To The
Sky By
The
Dynamic
Hologram
Of Jesus
Christ

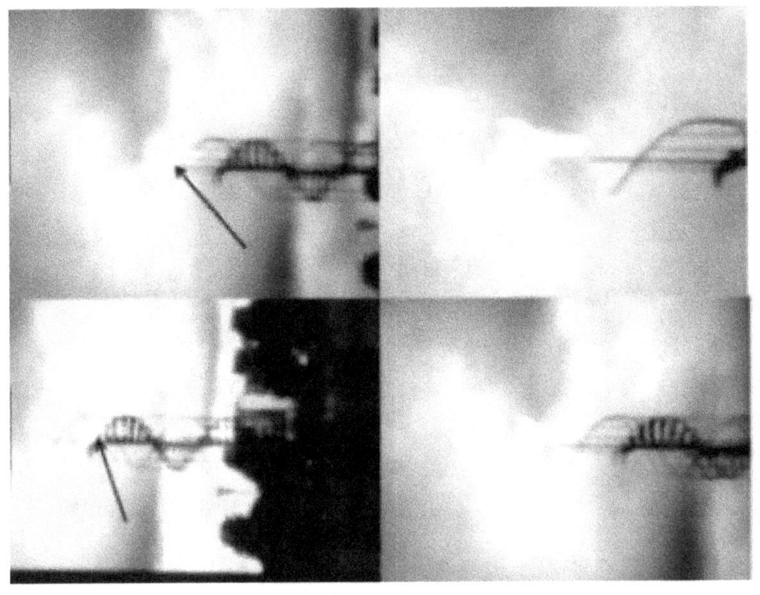

Dynamic Hologram Of Jesus Christ Flying From A Snail Ladder To The Sky

Dynamic Hologram Of Jesus Christ
Flying Over A Forest Ground

A Dynamic hologram on ground sent for Jesus Christ knocked a door of a woman at night she opened she find this:

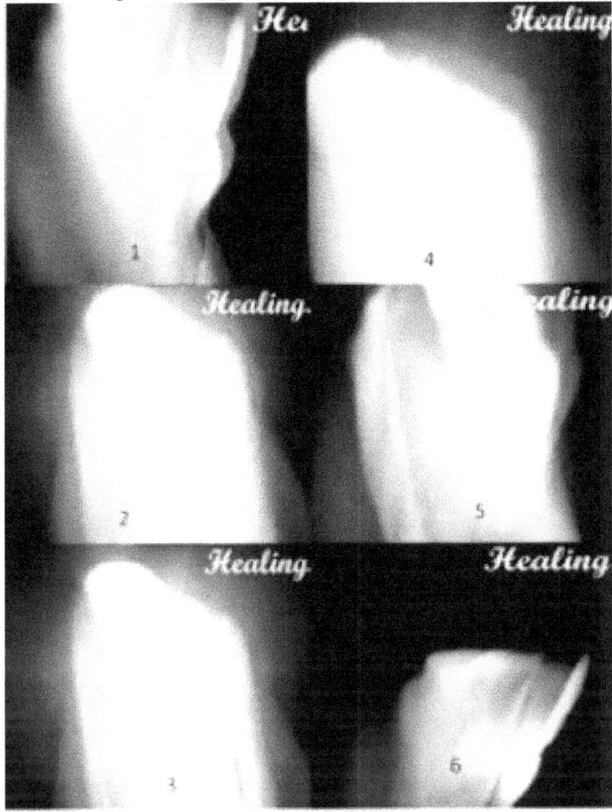

Dynamic Hologram pretented to be For Jesus Christ Knocking The Door at Night For A Woman

For The Muslims they sent and still sending religious holograms tailored with their beliefs and thoughts in this way they'll accept them easily and their reaction is and will be similar to Christians, Jews, Hindus and Buddhists : The God sent us these symbols to tell us that we are in the right path and we have a special position.

The 33 Degree Freemasons sent to Muslims a giant bird or Angel in their most sacred place on earth, The Kaaba, Home of Allah or God on earth built by Adam then rebuilt by Abraham or Ibrahim in Arabic language and his son Ismail. This dynamic hologram was sent in 2008 in Mecca the holiest Muslims 'city Worldwide.

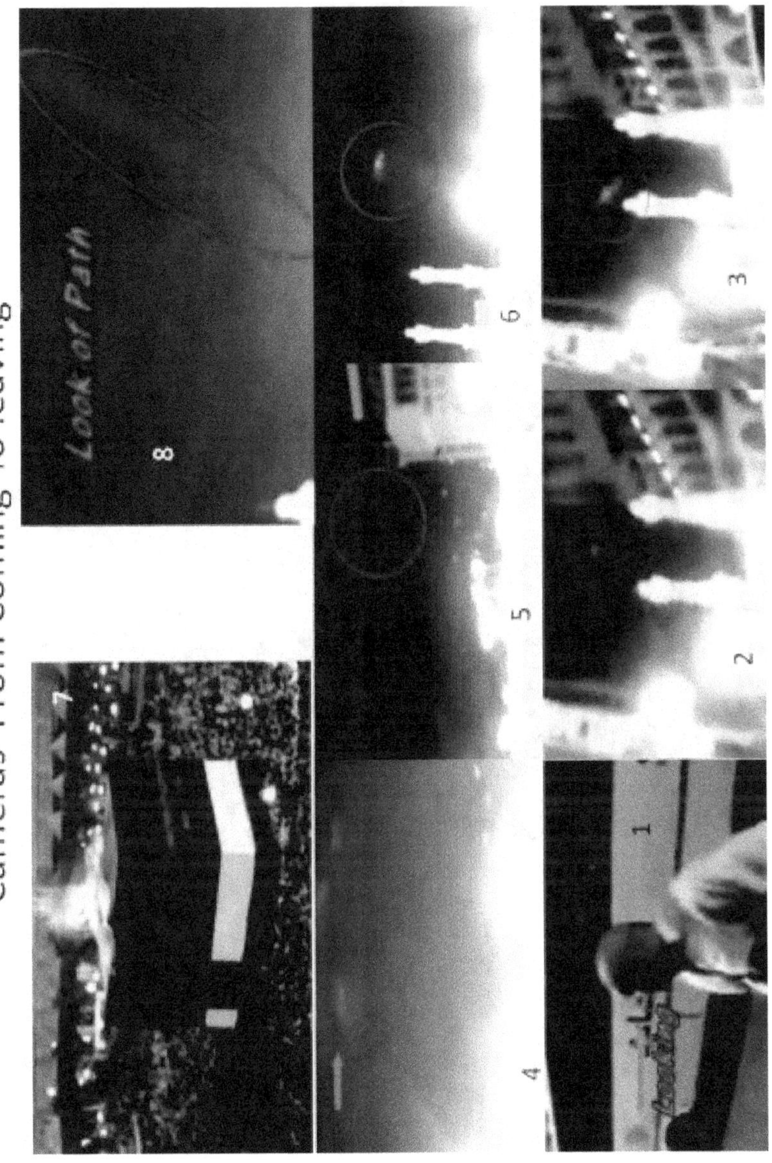

The Different Steps where The Giant Bird Captured By The Cameras From Coming To leaving

The Dynamic Hologram Of A Giant White Bird Considered As A White Angel By Some Muslims Over The Kaaba The Most Sacred Place

Another Angel or white bird dynamic hologram sent over the Dome Mosque in AlQuds(Jerusalem) in Palestine .It was in 2013 in the 25 th Night of Ramadan the holy Muslims month. A Palestinian called Mohamed Karim who recorded the video he stated that he remarked the Angel two days after the record when he review it to uploaded it to Youtube.

The Dome Mosque has great place in Muslims hearts as through it prophet Muhammad(SWS) did "Almaaraj" that means he flied to the seventh heaven. In this voyage he met several prophets like : Adam, Moses, Joseph, Jesus Christ, Abraham or Ibrahim, etc. Gabriel or Jibril the Saint Spirit who is the messenger of God to prophets was with him. He did this travel after he's coming from Mecca in the same night. This was miraculous that's why the unbelievers at that time disbelieved him despite he described for them all the details.

Other dynamic holograms like the horses were sent to different Muslims' countries the well known location one was in Jeddah Saudi Arabia filmed in a cloudy day(The horses has great symbolism for Muslims and Arabs. It's taken as a symbol of a coming triumph):

A Dynamic Horse Hologram Filmed In A Cloudy Sky From A Building In Jeddah Saudi Arabia

The horses appeared too in South Eastern of Asia mostly in Muslim countries like Indonesia, Pakistan or Malaysia.

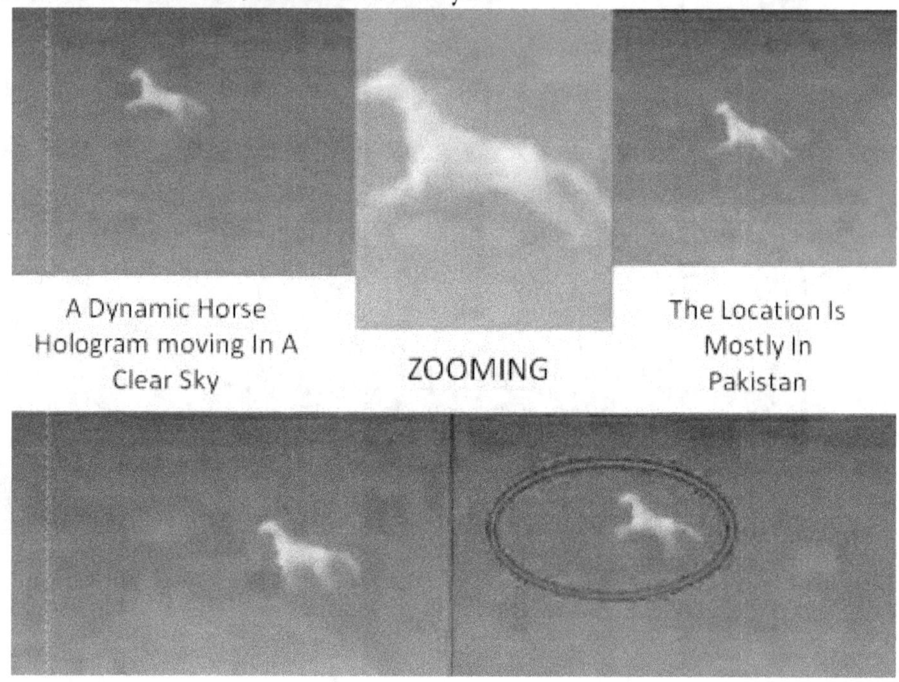

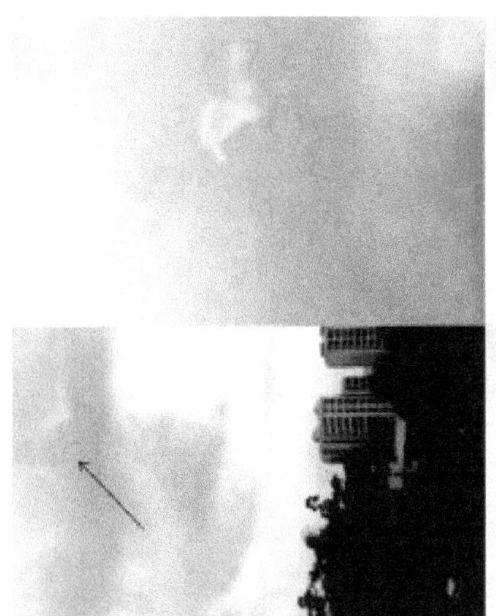

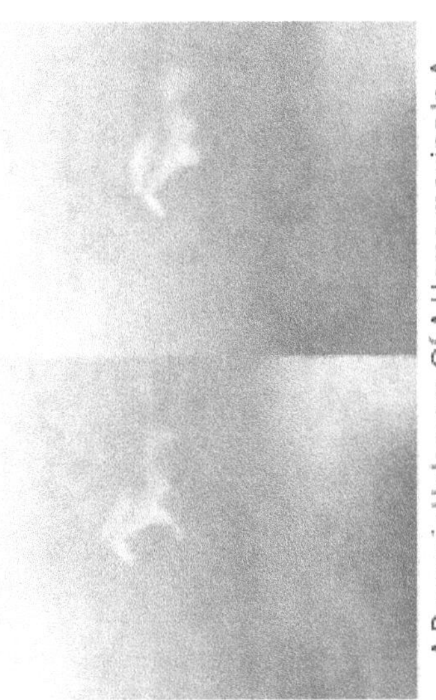

A Dynamic Hologram Of A Horse moving In A Cloudy Sky Over A South Eastern Muslim Country

Static Holograms for the name of prophet Muhammad(SWS) seen in Tunisia and Turkey:

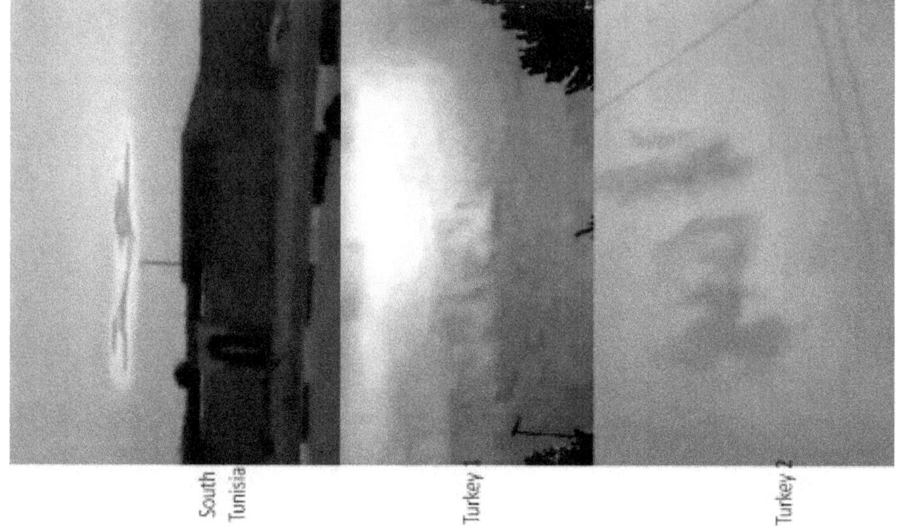

The name of prophet Muhammad(SWS) in Saudi Arabia, Egypt and Jordan:

Medina
(Saudi
Arabia)
Egypt
Jordan

The name of prophet Muhammud(SWS) in unknown locations:

The Static hologram of Allah which is the main name of God of Muslims seen too in different countries. In Morocco for example the name appeared several times in several locations like in the Rabat city, the capital.

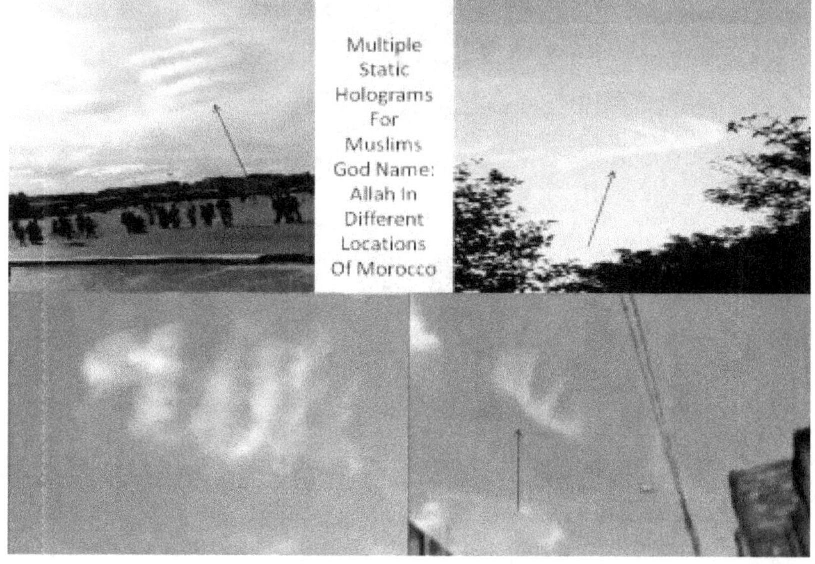

Mecca in Saudi Arabia, Syria, Tunisia and Turkey where the holograms appeared too.

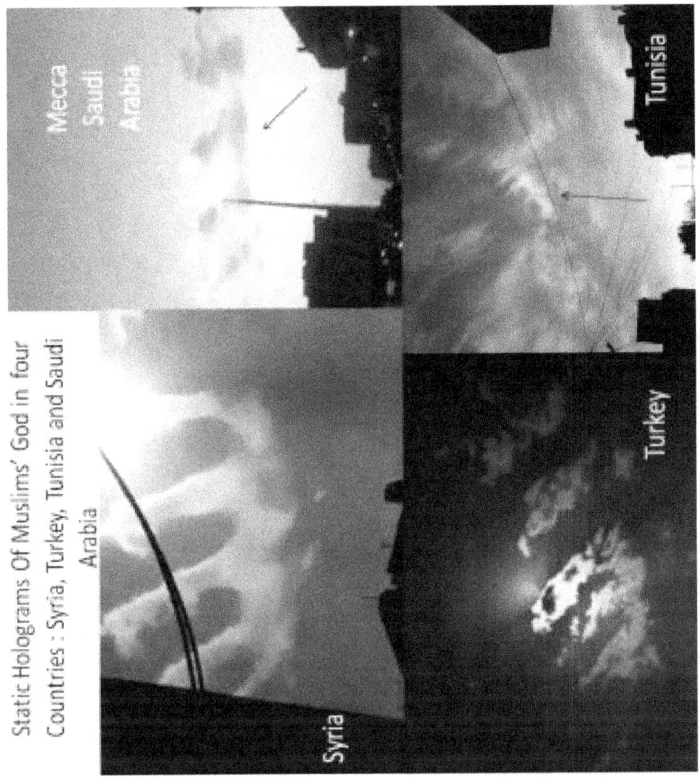

Static Holograms Of Muslims' God in four Countries : Syria, Turkey, Tunisia and Saudi Arabia

Other unknown locations:

The 33 degree Freemasons sent too a static hologram of a man doing his prayer(Salat in Arabic) :

A Static
Hologram
As a
Muslim
doing his
daily
Prayer

Another static hologram in the form of a Mosque sent in Saudi Arabic connected to a light it can be the sun on sunset or it's just a ball of light:

Under the step 4 for the supernatural manifestations on the ground too, they sent to the Muslims worldwide angels in the Mosques. As example a dynamic hologram of a supposed Angel assisted to a "khotba" of Jomoaa which is a weekly religious conference followed by a prayer done every Friday in the Mosques worldwide.

The record was live by the Saudi Arabia television station specialized in Sunnah Nabawya which is all what prophet Muhammad (SWS) said and did in his daily life something taken as reference and idol for Muslims worldwide in their lives. One of known Sunnah behavior as example is wearing the white color as the prophet Muhammad(SWS) preferred always the white color.

Another dynamic hologram for a supposed Angel too in a Mosque in Azrebaijan doing prayer:

For The Muslims Shia they sent them holograms like the name of Hussein the grand-son of prophet Muhammad(SWS) and his face on the moon projected(you remark here that they're interested in details for every religion, they know that Muslim Shia adores Hussein):

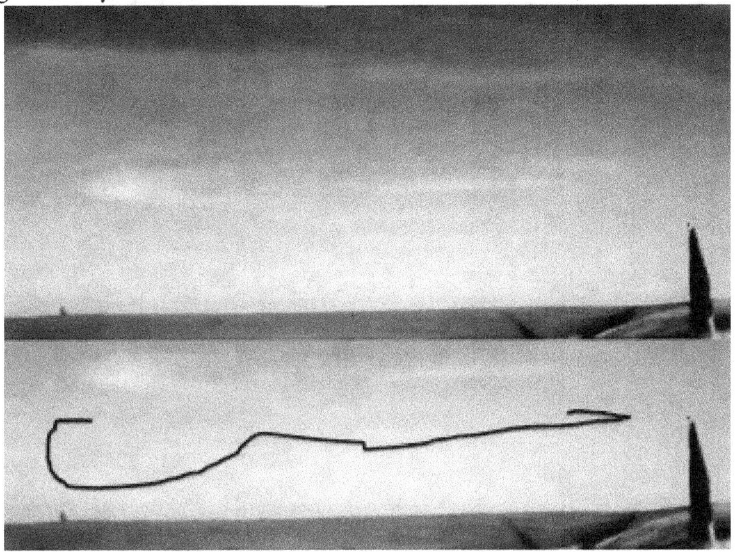

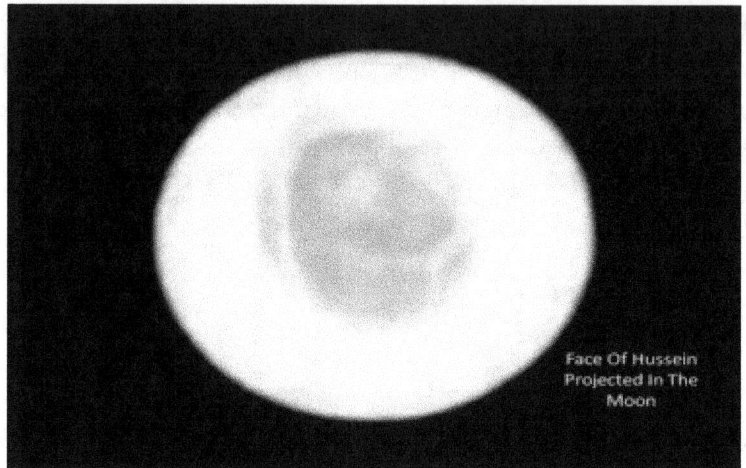
Face Of Hussein
Projected In The
Moon

On the ground they sent to Shia Muslims the dynamic hologram representing Fatima AlZahraa the daughter of prophet Muhammad(SWS) and the mother of beheaded Hussein in a Husseinite in karbala (In Iraq) the city where Hussein was betrayed and killed:

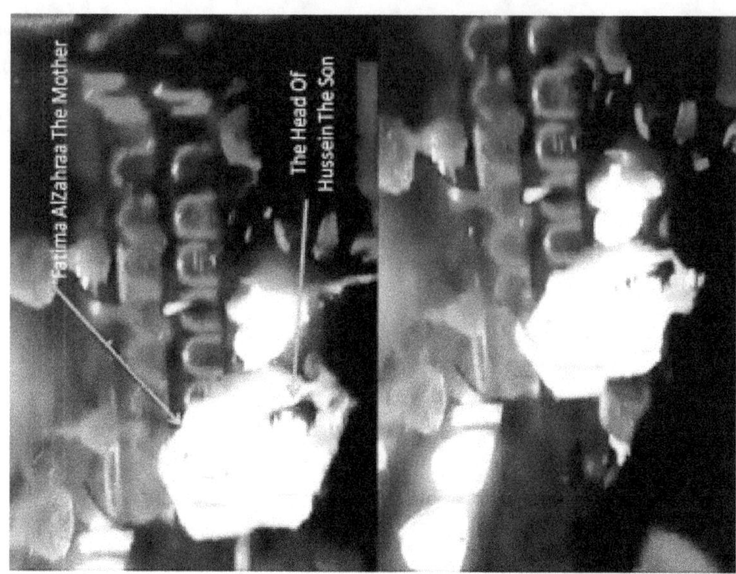

Dynamic Hologram Of Fatima AlZahraa Carrying The Head Of Hussein Her Son. She beat Her Head As An Expression Of Sadness

Another dynamic hologram on ground sent to Shia Muslims this time in Iran with the personality of "AlAbbas" Who was the brother of Hussein he tried to bring water to his brother Hussein and his family as the betrayals cut the water from them.

Shia Muslims Think That This is AlAbbass Brother Of Hussein

For the Buddhists, Buddha holograms were and still presents in different countries where Buddha is worshipped .It appeared in Thailand in a cloudy day:

In a blue clear sky Buddha hologram was present:

Clear Static Hologram Of Buddha In Philippines

A hologram for a sacred mummified Monk appeared in the sky without noise as it's specificity for the mummified monks in Buddhism religion:

Near a Buddhism community, appeared a hologram of Buddha in the sky:

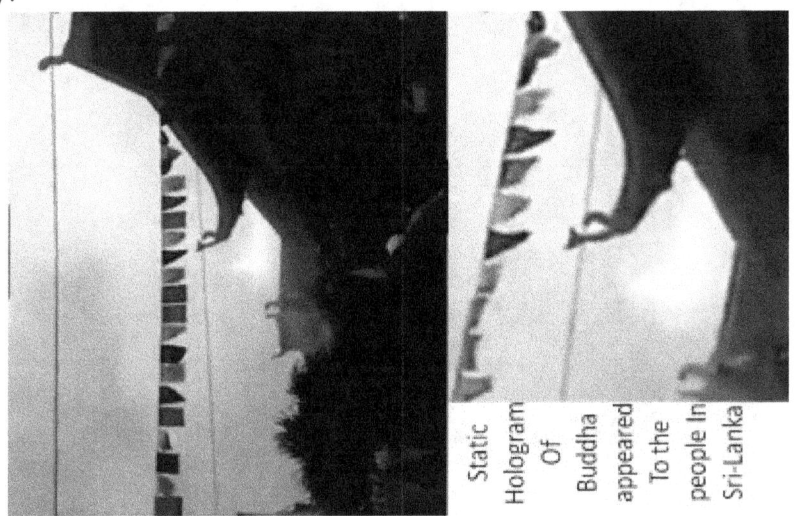

A static hologram for a Buddha sleeping on his dorsal in the sky

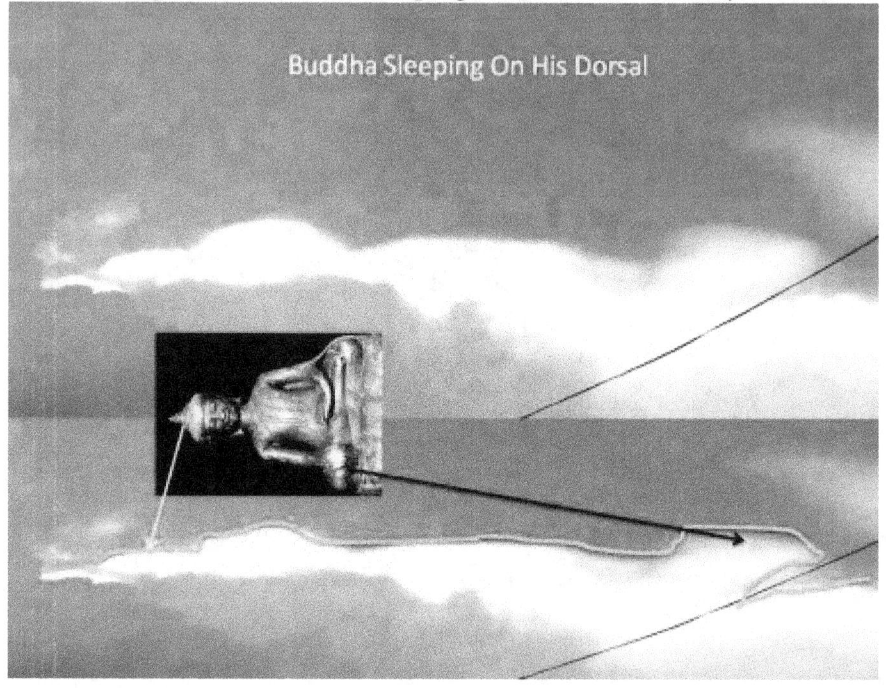

A hologram for a Buddha sleeping on his left shoulder:

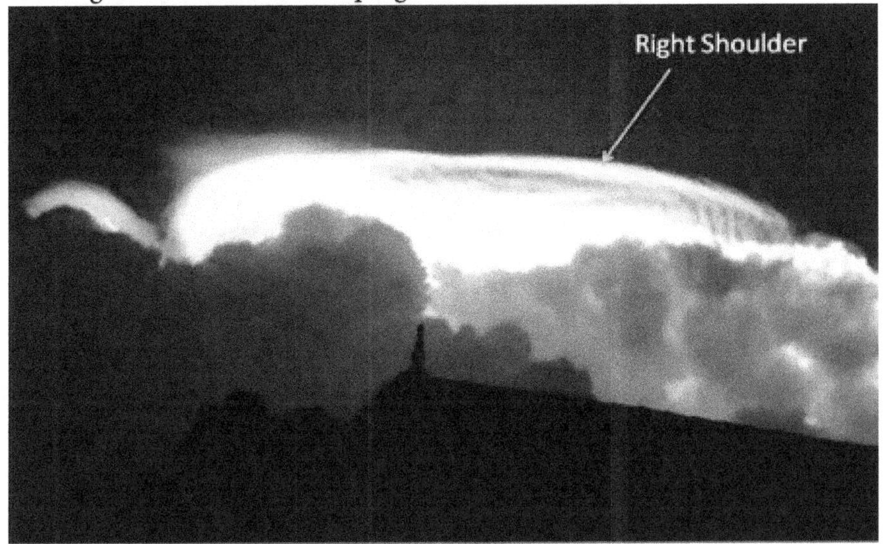

Static Hologram Of Buddha Sleeping On His Left Shoulders

In China, they sent to Buddhists ancient cities floating over the clouds, this city is related in memory with ancient cities of Buddha or sacred monks.

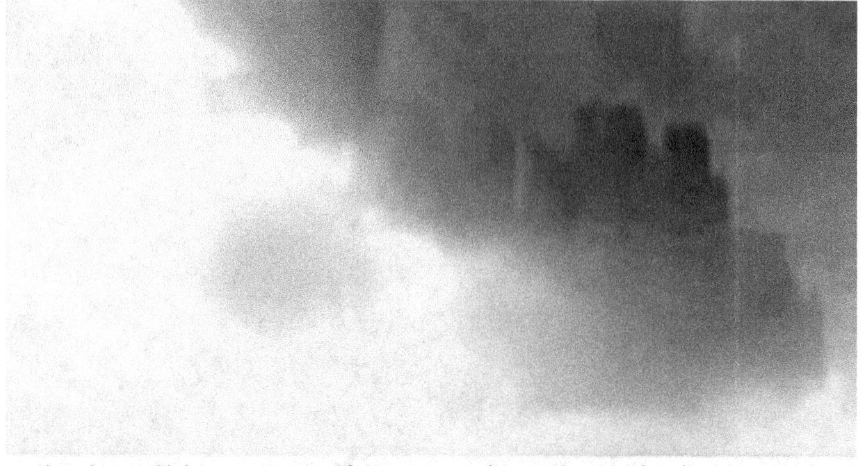

Ancient Cities sent to Chinese making them thinking about Buddha ancient and sacred days.

Nowadays you'll find television reports about the mirage or reflection of cities in the clouds it's even reported in CNN, it's not true, the 33 degree freemasons did these cities as the modern ones to give the impression that it's a reflection and has no relation with their project the project blue beam.

They need more time to cover their real intentions as their criminal agenda is becoming more and more recognized worldwide. They intentionally do this to disperse the concentration of people. For example this image show a reflection of buildings and cranes in an eastern Chinese Shandong province city called Yantai:

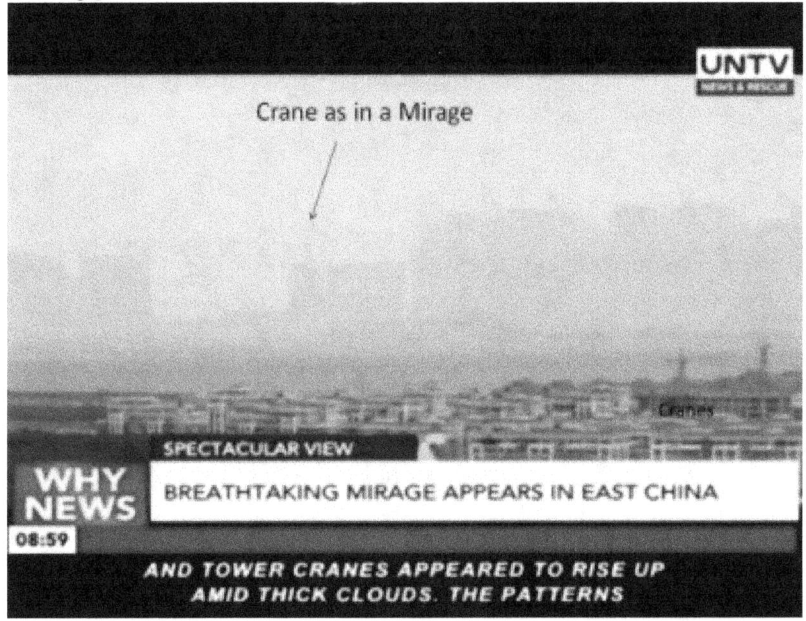

Ancient city was sent to UK, mostly it's the ancient city of Jerusalem it was sent to England as a thank you way as UK gave Palestine with its capital Jerusalem to the Rothschild family as the first entity for building Greater Israel Kingdom.

Static Hologram Of Ancient city Of Jerusalem, AlQuds or Orschalim over UK Sky

To believe more that all what you read and see is not a conspiracy theory and this is unfortunately true and those people are real criminals and don't waste time, look to the next series of images taken from a smart phone recording a monster or a dragon ascending to the sky and entered in the clouds.

The message to Chinese : Corona virus is gone from China, this small film was recorded in March 19th 2020 when Corona virus was really begin leaving China despite persisting in other countries as China mission is over for this virus.

It can be for China or Japan a static hologram showing mystic creatures like Angel with wings, animal with horns people talking side by side, it's like an artistic work but with strange voices:

A Static Hologram
For Mystic creatures
like Angels with
wings animals with
horns,etc

For The Hinduism Followers a Static Hologram for a Senior Monk seen in the sky :

The 33 degree Freemasons sent also dynamic holograms to terrorize people worldwide in the air and in the sea. For example a dynamic hologram of a dragon like watched in cinema was captured with video in the island of Llios in Greece in August the 5th 2018, watch the sequence of images and how the dragon hologram was assembled at the end:

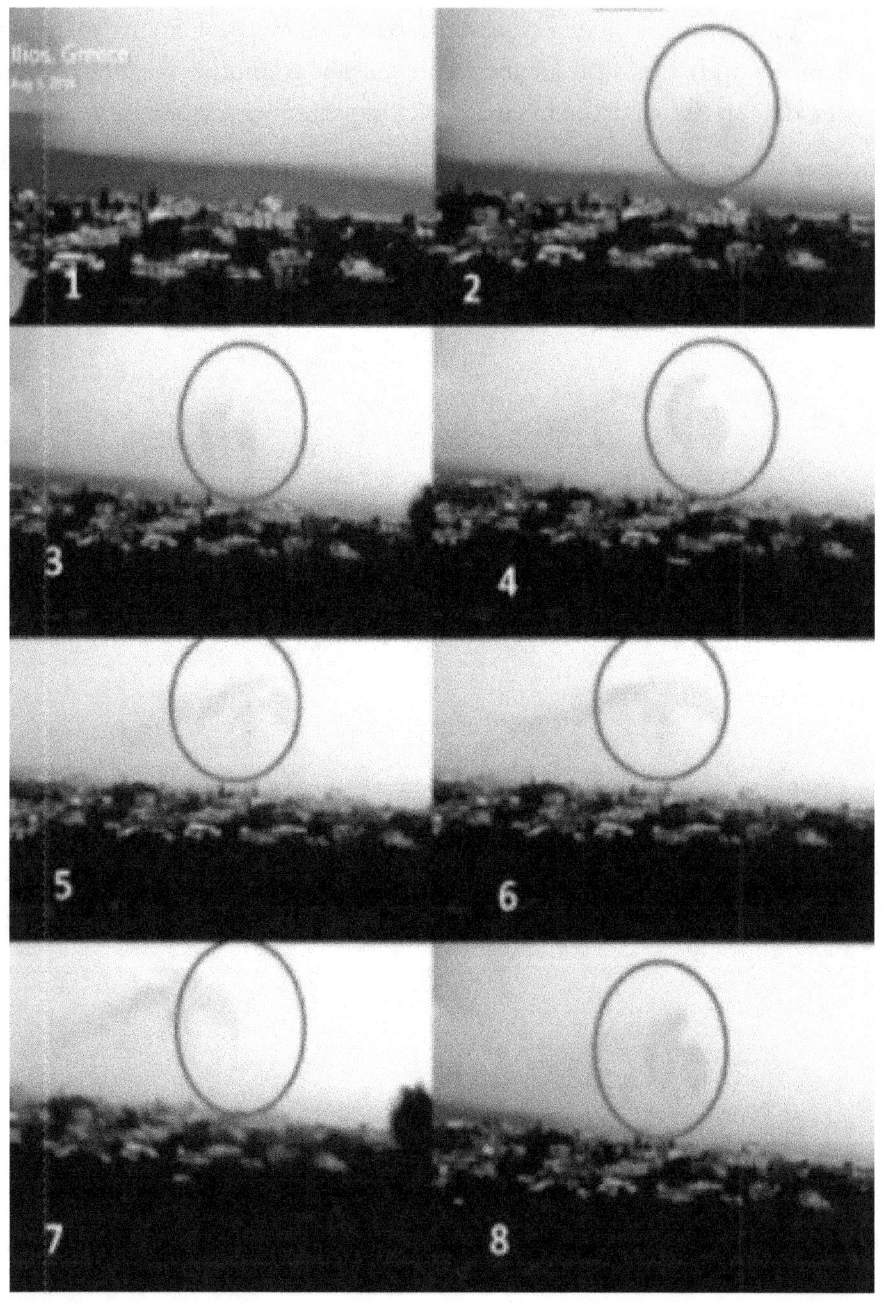

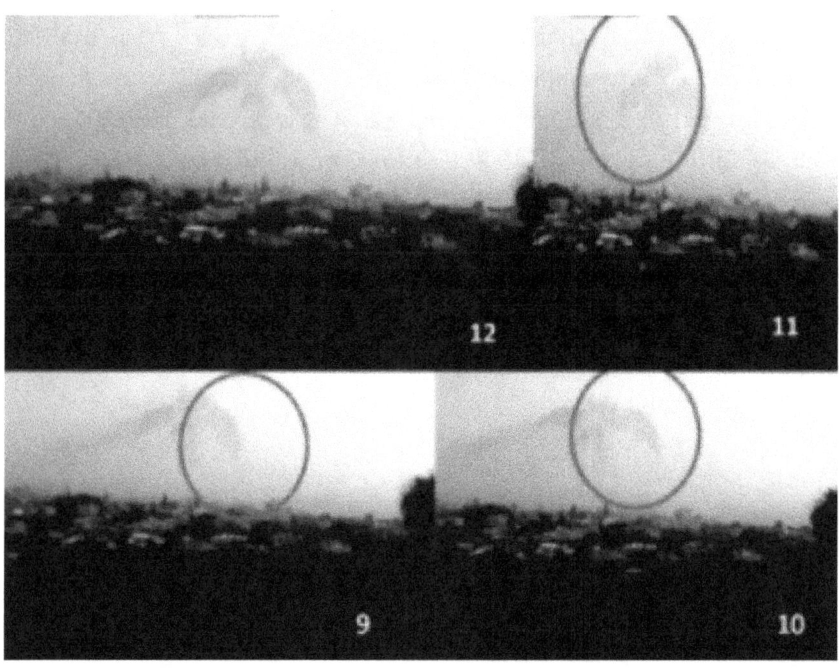

They sent too another dynamic hologram of a duck with frightening eyes, two balls of fire mostly are Nazis UFOs as I said the Nazis UFOs can be transformed to a ball of fire or light as it was recorded by the US Navy in High Jump Operation in 1947.Concentrate in huge size of the hologram, the movement of the eyes and the magical control of the sight, watching to front, then to his left then to his down and finally to his right and before all that it was one light ball then appeared the second in a cloudy thunder-flash lightening atmosphere and surely this climate state is made by them or by the collaboration with another team:

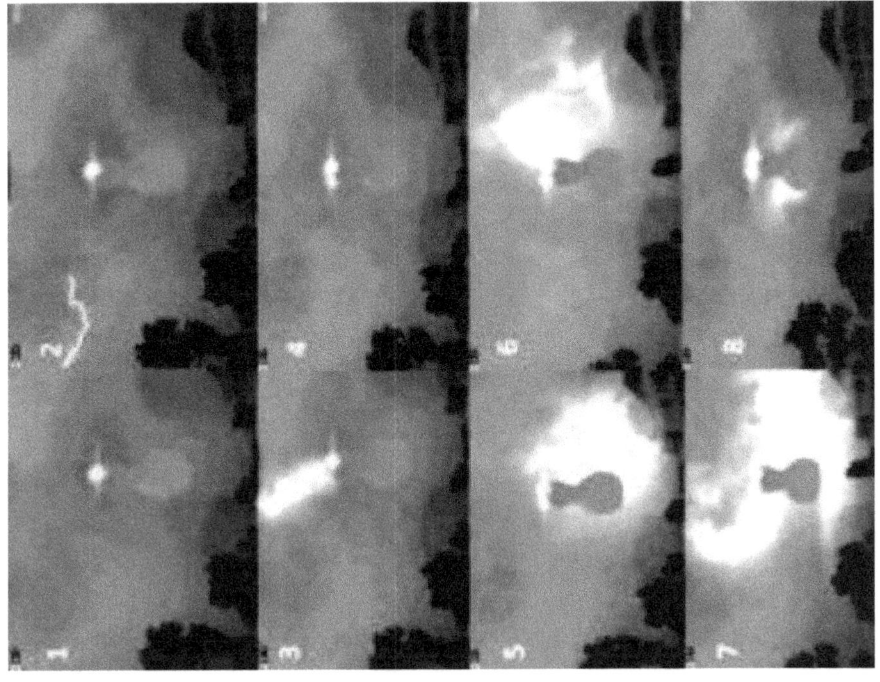

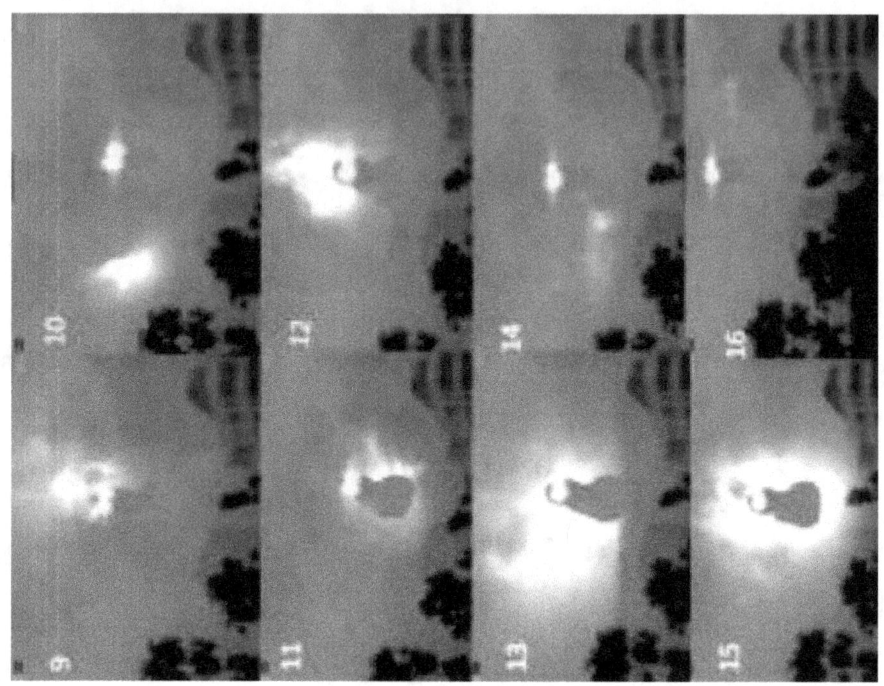

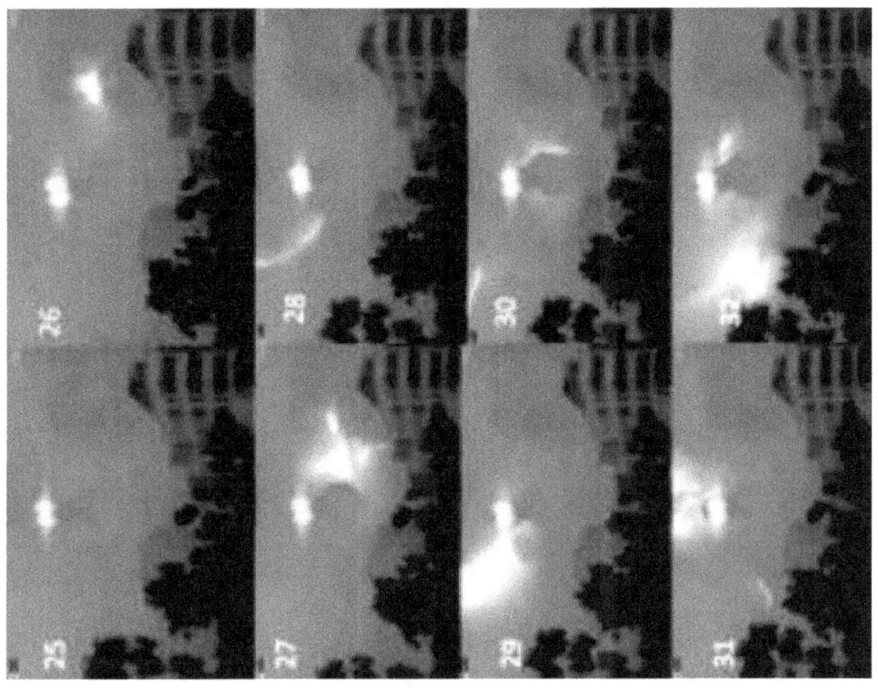

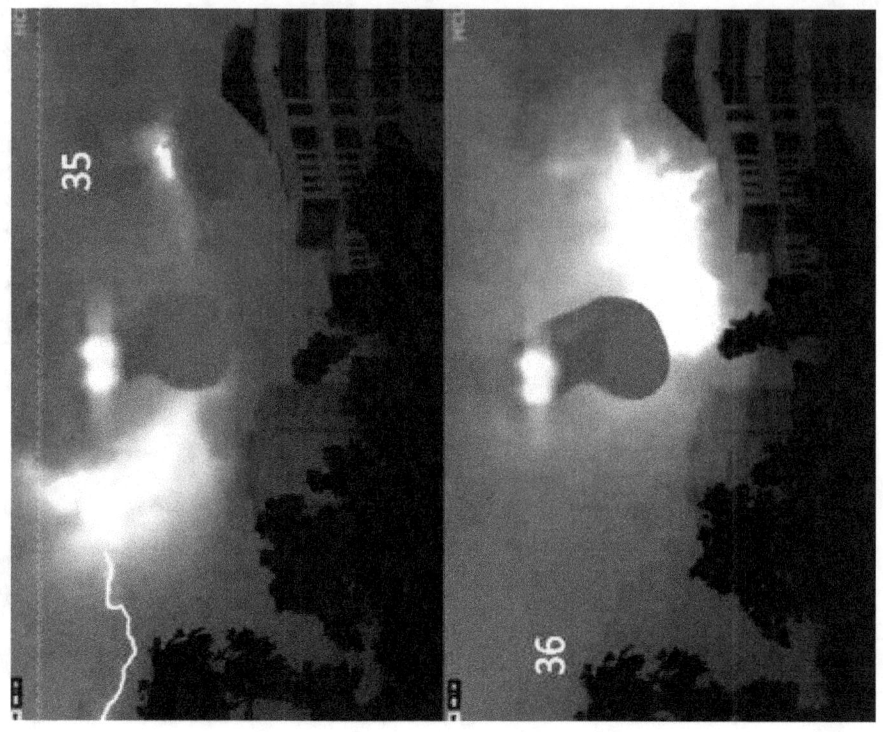

To terrorize people in the sea as the great show will not be just in the air, a huge sneak with head of a human king with a beard and a crown:

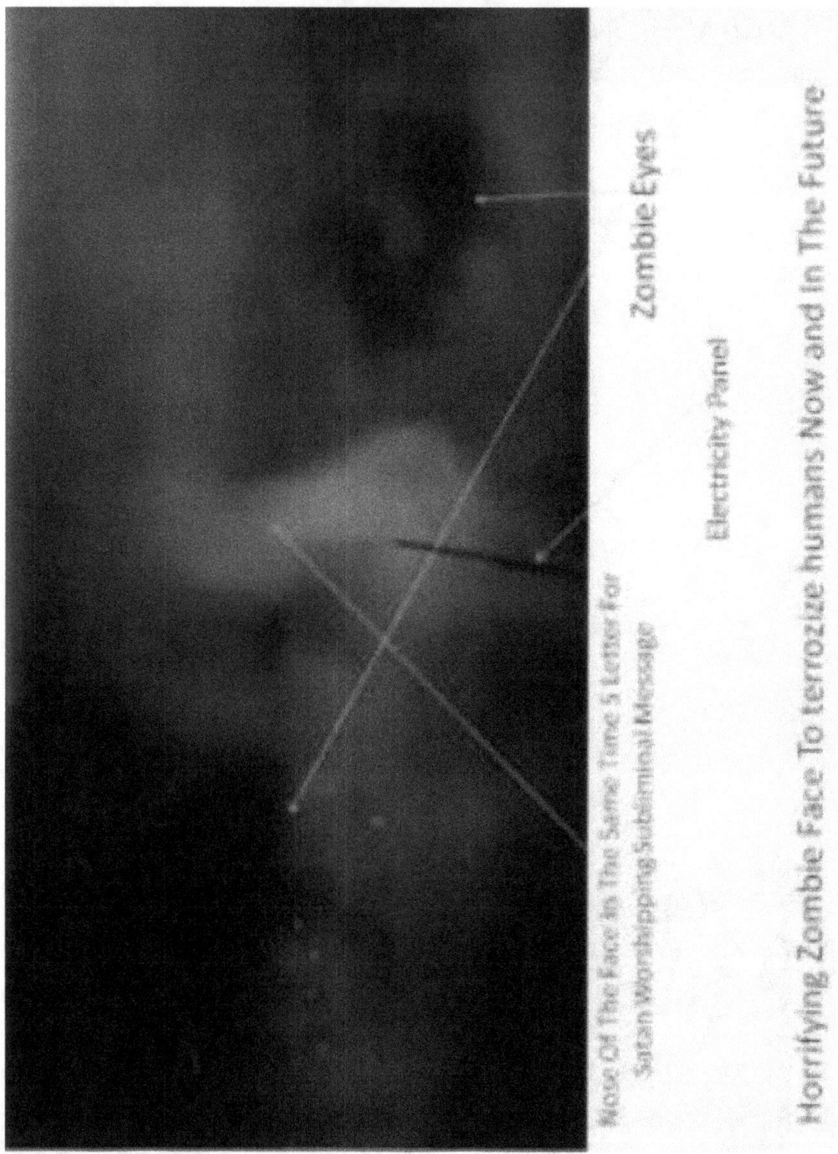

A face of a Zombie with black eyes and a Nose with "S" letter to the Satan made in the sky to terrify people

C.10: Strange Voices heard Worldwide

In the last twenty years, strange voices were and still heard in almost all countries worldwide, some thought that they are coming from the Big Bang Explosion from 14 Billion years despite that it's just a theory, some think that they are coming from the hollow earth theory some think it's natural coming from interactions between waves including all different kinds from cell phones, to television to radio to military to space, etc that's means they are natural and spontaneous.

In reality, those voices or sounds are for me just tests for the sound effects that will be used in the fake Aliens invasion process with all its steps. Those sounds will glorify the experience of watching the great show of the flying saucers or UFOs which they will be very huge even with hundreds of kilometers as diameters.

Those voices will be used as bombs effects, destruction effects to terrorize people worldwide. What we hear is just calibration of the sounds like anyone do in a party before its starting he try to check the volume, the levels and types of the voices.

Those voices are made principally by the HAARP project (High-Frequency Active Auroral Reseach Program). They're one of its main functions beside the weather manipulation including storms, the earth quakes, the volcano eruptions incitement and the sinkholes made.

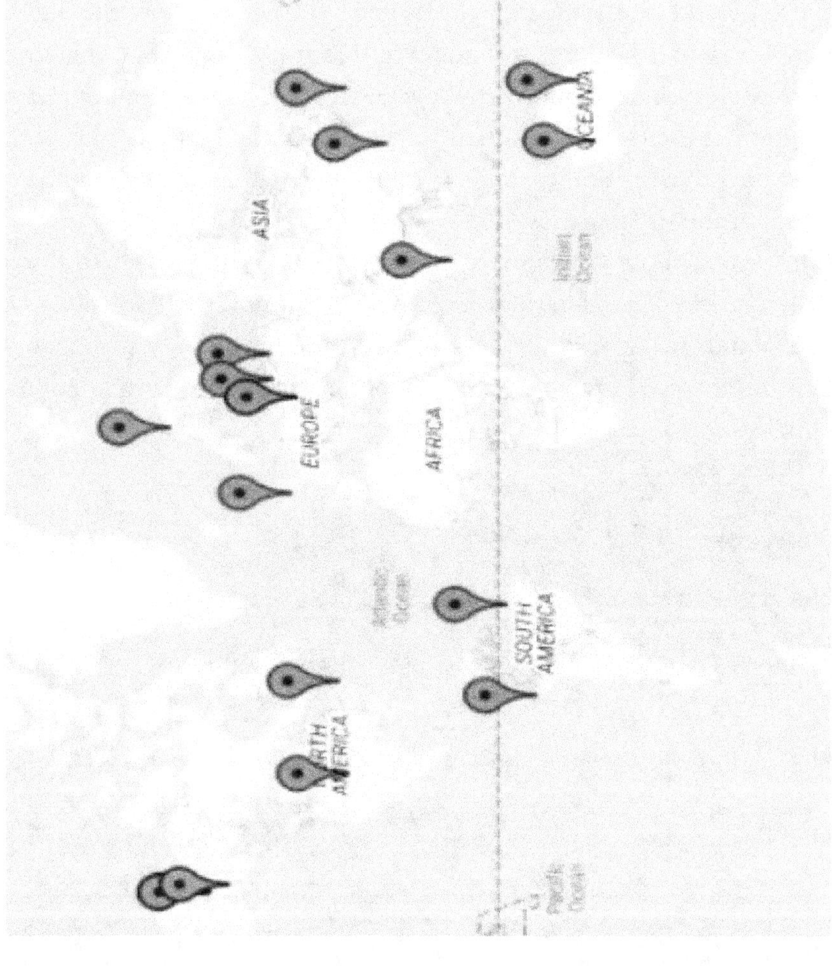

If you remark, you see that voices are heard worldwide without exceptions that's why HAARP has so many stations implanted but under different names firstly to camouflage their real missions and secondly even who work on them still ignorant about that, it's the same system for workers and officials in NASA and her sisters, in intelligence structures like CIA and MI6 and in some secret bases like Area 51 and S4.Everyone has a planned tasks that he or she accomplish without knowing anything about other colleagues tasks.

In 2015, The HAARP property transferred to Alaska University to give the sensation that it's a civilian facility. It was founded and still belonging to the US Air Force, US Navy and The Defense Advanced Research Projects Agency (DARPA).The builder or the contractor of all its systems is BAE Advanced Technology specialized in military systems!

Think a moment, all the involved parts are militaries, do you still believe that it's a civilian research tool or what is already talking about the criminal use of HARP project is a conspiracy theory?

Now, they said and declared that HAARP is the most powerful high Frequencies Transmitter to the Ionosphere not a receiver! That's means HAARP send Frequencies and waves to the ionosphere layer via The Ionospheric Research Instrument (IRI) on a specified area to excite it as they states. Then the reflection of frequencies returns to the facility to be analyzed (here think about a signal of light reflected in a mirror).

In the materials physics techniques of characterization when you apply any kind of force which can be frequencies on any area of a material, automatically this force will change the physical properties of this material so it can't return to its initial state before the applied force or incitement it's called: "The equilibrium state or state of equilibrium".

So even we consider the good intention side for HAARP project this IRI changed and still changing the physical properties of the specified ionosphere studied areas for decades now! And this is a crime against the earth, the atmosphere, the environment, the humans and the animals. None has the right to change or manipulates the atmosphere composition state, people must move legally against this project and who is really behind it(The 33 Degree Free masons).

The road of the high frequencies to the ionosphere pass by the first layers of the atmosphere: Troposphere, Stratosphere and Mesosphere. These layers in all the means and ways their physical properties are changing every time. Even the specified excited areas are just in Alaska as they pretends, this is affects the entire atmosphere worldwide as HAARP works now for 30 years.

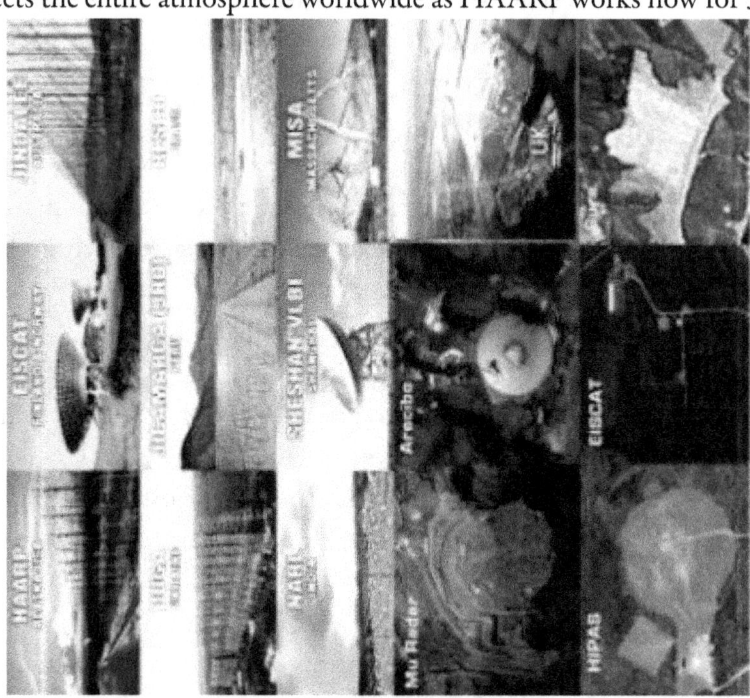

The Frequencies produced and sent coming from an Alternative Current not a Direct Current something is very harsh.

Think if we apply for example different frequencies in the same area for recurrent periods of time, is that will not affects the atmosphere layers so not affect the climate? What's about the reflections and refractions?

In this scenario HAARP cannot be an innocent tool.

Some of The main HAARP Capabilities:

-Generating very low frequency (VLF) radio waves by modulated heating of the auroral electrojet: remark here heating.

-Generating artificial Airglow, under certain geophysical conditions and transmitter configurations, it can be bright enough to see it with the naked eye: The artificial Airglow is very effective in the holograms formation in the sky sent to different religions followers worldwide.

-VLF remote sensing of the heated ionosphere: heated ionosphere equal to damaged ionosphere.

HAARP Research Observations:

-Plasma line observations

-Stimulated electron emission observations: This is one of main changing physical properties applied forces on the atmosphere layers.

-Gyro frequency heating research: heating the frequency of a moving charged particles in a magnetic field in the ionosphere something strongly changes its physical properties so its nature.

-Heating induced scintillation observations

-VLF and ELF (Extremely Low Frequency) generation observations

-Radio observations of meteors: this is the cover for many other HAARP stations like in Peru.

-Polar mesospheric summer echoes (PMSE) have been studied, probing the mesosphere using the IRI as a powerful radar, and with a 28 MHz radar and two VHF radars at 49 MHz and 139 MHz: this can be taken as the elevation of earth temperature as they spread it in their mainstream media, the global warming.

-Testing of Spread Spectrum Transmitters : it can be used in holograms creation.

Meteor shower impacts on the ionosphere: this can be analyzed as I know they'll make a real meteor shower on earth to kill maximum of people, making a third world war as the fossil sources of energy like oil and gas wells will be destroyed and to exhausts the humanity to easily accept the fake aliens invasion as a reality.

-Producing high density plasma clouds in Earth's upper atmosphere: This too can be analyzed as a tool to creates the holograms based on the clouds and also the storms creations, the heavy clouds for heavy rains and floods in weather manipulation.

-Underground imaging: it can be used for mines search to control them worldwide and it can be for the use of dynamic holograms on ground like Jesus for Christians on the river, Mary The Virgin in Church, The angel White Bird for Muslims and the lady Zinab for Mullims' Shia.

Research conducted at the HAARP facility has allowed the US military to perfect communications with its fleet of submarines by sending radio signals over long distances.

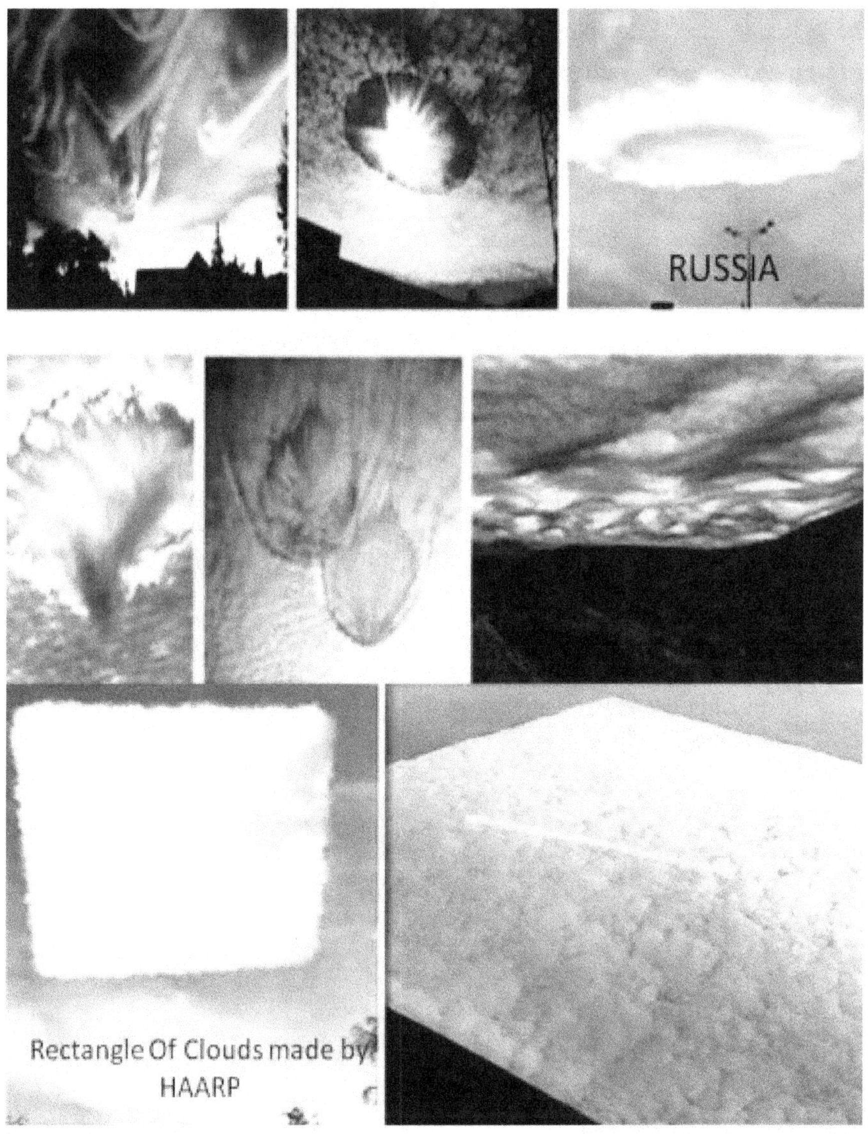

Some Doings Of HAARP Project Worldwide

Below two examples of the step 4 of the blue beam project the supernatural manifestations:

C.11: Sky Chemicals & Secret Projects

Chemtrails are artificial lines of chemicals in the atmosphere pulverized by civil airplanes worldwide .

The composition with nanoscopic and picoscopic dimensions vary from aluminum to barium. Its spread in the air from the criminals of this world the 33 degree Freemasons and their slaves doing their missions without being aware of the gravity and danger, it has multiple targets: contamination of the faune and flore so contamination of the complete ecosystem including humans and animals so cancers, more illnesses, genetic influence on new born generations then big Pharma big sales, more insurances money, etc.

The second target is helping the projection of holograms in the air by chemical reactivity between the atmosphere ingredients.

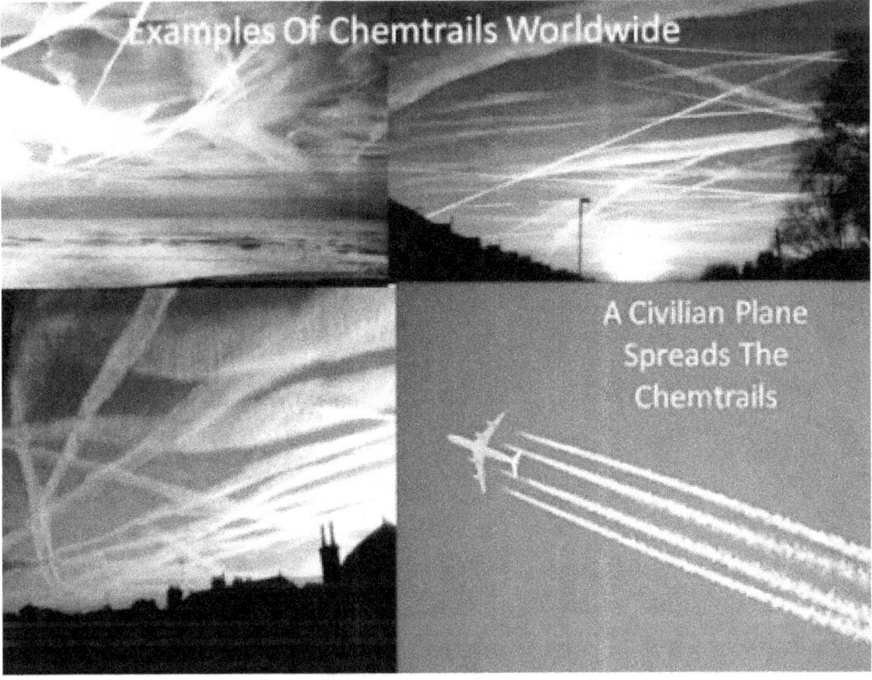

After the world war 2, USA and its allies applied so many secret experiences most of them were on weather control and the atmosphere manipulation. In August 15, 1952, an experiment in South England occurred, so many planes flied to make a weather modification, the result was a huge rainfall, killing thousands and millions of pounds as losses. The British defense minister deny completely the experience.

In 1958, the US Navy exploded three fission type nuclear bombs 480 km above the South Atlantic Ocean, in the part of the lower Van Allen Belt closest to the earth's surface. In addition, two hydrogen bombs were detonated 160 km over Johnston Island in the Pacific. This was called, by the military, "the biggest scientific experiment ever undertaken".

It was designed by the US Department of Defense and the US Atomic Energy Commission, under the code name Project Argus.

The purpose was to assess the impact of high altitude nuclear explosions on radio transmission and radar operations because of the electromagnetic pulse (EMP), and to increase understanding of the geomagnetic field and the behavior of the charged particles in it.

In 1962, the US began a new series of experiences with the ionosphere. "one kiloton device, at a height of 60 km and one megaton and one multi-megaton, at several hundred kilometers height".

These tests seriously disturbed the lower Van Allen Belt, substantially altering its shape and intensity. "In this experiment the inner Van Allen Belt will be practically destroyed for a period of time; particles from the Belt will be transported to the atmosphere. It is anticipated that the earth's magnetic field will be disturbed over long distances for several hours, preventing radio communication.

The explosion in the inner radiation belt created an artificial dome of polar light that will be visible from Los Angeles." These experiments were under the name of "Project Starfish".

In 1966, a project called "Popeye" was in place it was an experiment in increased rainfall through cloud seeding jointly approved by the U.S. Department of State and U.S. Department of Defense. The technical aspects of the experiment were verified by Dr. Donald F. Hornig, Special Assistant to the President of the United States for Science and Technology. The government of Laos was not informed of the project, its methods or its goals.

Robert S. McNamara, U.S. Secretary of Defense, was aware that there might be objections raised by the international scientific community but said in a memo to the president that such objections had not in the past been a basis for prevention of military activities considered to be in the interests of U.S. national security.

During October 1966, Project Popeye was tested in a strip of the Laos panhandle east of the Bolovens Plateau in the Se Kong River valley. The test was conducted by personnel from the Naval Ordnance Test Station located at China Lake California. Fifty cloud seeding experiments were conducted with the result that 82% of the clouds produced rain within a brief period after having been seeded.

It was claimed that one of the clouds drifted across the Vietnam border and dropped nine inches of rain on a US special forces camp over a four hour period. After the successful completion of the test phase, Project Popeye transitioned from an experiment to an operational program of the U.S. Defense department.

Operation Popeye goal was to increase rainfall and extend the monsoon season specifically over areas of the Ho Chi Minh Trail in carefully selected area as to deny the Vietnamese enemy, namely military supply trucks, the use of roads by: Softening road surfaces, Causing landslides along roadways, Washing out river crossings and maintain saturated soil conditions beyond the normal time span.

In 1985, an innovative use of the Space Shuttle to perform space physics experiments in earth orbit was launched, using the OMS injections of gases to "cause a sudden depletion in the local plasma concentration, the creation of a so called ionospheric hole".

This artificially induced plasma depletion can then be used to investigate other space phenomena, such as the growth of the plasma instabilities or the modification of radio propagation paths.

The 47 second OMS burn of July 29, 1985, produced the largest and most long lived ionospheric hole to date, dumping some 830 kg of exhaust into the ionosphere at sunset. A 6 second, 68 km OMS release above Connecticut in August 1985, produced an airglow which covered over 400,000 square km.During the 1980's rocket launches globally numbered about 500 to 600 a year, peaking at 1500 in 1989.

There were many more during the Gulf War. The Shuttle is the largest of the solid fuel rockets, with twin 45 meter boosters. All solid fuel rockets release large amounts of hydrochloric acid in their exhaust, each Shuttle flight injecting about 75 tones of ozone destroying chlorine into the stratosphere.

Those launched since 1992 inject even more ozone destroying chlorine, about 187 tones, into the stratosphere (which contains the ozone layer).

These secret experiences are some of leaked ones, so many others still in secrecy. The most important thing is the conspiracy theory opinion is not accepted yet we have real conspiracies by real men.

C.12: Weaponized Satellites

Satellites were and are essential parts of Blue Beam Project and the fake Aliens invasions different steps .We ignore when and how these Satellites were and are put in their orbits.

We heard in mainstream media news about rockets sent to orbit to put satellites for specific missions like communication, television and radio, spying, weather, military, etc

The big question is if the mainstream media give the right information, which of those satellites are used in the holography and Blue Beam Project? And if this media lies, the satellites are really sent via rockets or they are just put in orbits thanks to the human made flying saucers including the Nazis ones!

We have two scenarios here, the first one is that the specified satellites are sent by vertical rockets like the Russian Soyuz or the French Ariane (just remark here that this technology is from the Nazis era who were the first users of rockets thanks to engineers like the American space program manager Wernher Von Braun, that's means after a seven decades or seventy years of science development, the humanity stay in the phase of vertical Rockets launching from the fourteens era of the twentieth century even with Space X, Blue Origin and Virgin Galactic, they can't yet put satellites in low orbit!).

Here another question can be asked which is how they sent these kind of weapons into space without our knowledge despite every Rocket launch to space is covered by mainstream media and especially the NASA TV?

The answer is clear those satellites are as they described purposes : for Television, Radios, communication, weather, etc, but they have other non declared options beside their essential missions like for example the projection of electrons, photons, solar winds, electromagnetic waves, micro and nano waves to a specified areas on earth to change the climate or to make holograms or to send sounds beside the use as weapon by accumulating the solar energy and orients it as energy beam against any enemy on earth or in space.

Here I remember you about the Weaponization of the space told from Wernher Von Braun to Doctor Carol Rosin.

The second theory is that the specified satellites to the Blue Beam Project or other secret projects are just put in orbits thanks to human made UFOs naturally unseen by the entire humanity.

C.13: Civilian & Military Navy

The US Marine and NATO members ships are involved in the Blue beam project and other secret ones mostly without knowledge of the majority of army, the white house, government, congress and the president of United States .Their main role is using the developed technology in the ships for the service of those projects in the specified time .

Their role also consists in the protection of any requested secret operation when it's running, cooperates with the participant military submarines and other "commercial" ships which are owned by Free Masonry followers corporations and contains supplement high technological infrastructure designed to work in the defined date.

The submarines and ships can send some kinds of rockets into ionosphere or other sky layer to help making a projection of a hologram.

We should remember here that the industrial-military complex is one of greatest and principal arms of the Free Masonry cartel.

So it's very naturally that so many commercial, oil and gas transportation ships or any other kind of ships be involved in this great crime, even more there's no declared nuclear and sophisticated submarines constructed and owned by this cartel with knowledge of American army .

C.14: Private Properties Involved

The money can do anything and the 33 degree Freemasons are the greatest experts in this domain, they created Banks, insurances and corporations even they owned countries lands in the United States itself and other ones in the world, it will not be difficult to them to buy lands in different continents and make them secret bases and employ them to their causes like the Blue Beam Project.

Those secret bases are mostly great houses which can't be thought as a cover for secret programs.

Beside those hidden bases there's teams of researchers in universities laboratories are working for these causes and are paid for that perhaps the doctorate students did their Ph.D researches in the service of Blue Beam projects without their knowledge or acceptance.

Furthermore many private laboratories founded by the 33 degree Freemasons and paid very well are also an arm to this satanic project and other ones.

C.15: The Prepared Scenario

The scenario will be a meteors shower then a world war 3 then a fake aliens invasions, all these steps to depopulate the maximum of humans and exhausts the rest and finally the false Messiah appears in the sky talking to the rest of humans worldwide in the same time with every language for each country and people and even with tailored tongues for every community. This dynamic hologram will be with high definition quality very convincible in his speech.

This scenario was shown in a Japanese cartoon series called: "Nadia, The Secret Of Blue Water" in 1990.This cartoon is full with Freemasonry symbols like the eye, the pyramid, the triangle, the ground of the lodge full of squares, etc. The 33 degree Freemasons did this cartoon to program the kids generations about the future which will occurs, in this way their acceptance later in the reality will be easier.

This technique is well known in psychology under the "Subliminals" name. It was and still used by them in the movies, television series, documentaries, the news, etc.

One of a well known subliminals was in 1996 in the movies of Samuel L. Jackson, "The Long Kiss Goodnight" about the September 11th 2001 attacks when a member of the criminals said: "We hit the New York Twin Towers, we kill 3000 Americans then we say they were the Muslim Terrorists". This is what occurred exactly.

Here I should remember you that The Freemasonry has an age of 400 years old and it's infiltrated with secrecy in the entire world, they were the creators of the World Wars 1 and 2, they destroyed Japan and rebuilt it again with their agenda .

They pushed Japan, South Korea and Taiwan with technology meanwhile they programmed us that those countries are Dragons of South

East Asia, they developed for them the democracy and they protected and still those democracies from the military coup something which is the contrary in middle and south America, Africa and some of south east Asia countries like Indonesia!

They created and supported "military coups d'état" and changed complete democracies with favorable ones to their agendas. That's why you ask always the question why democracy don't succeed in some countries? The answer is what I said all what you see about the political discussions in mainstream media is for the masses manipulation not more.

I'll show you now the scenario prepared by them as they made in the cartoon. A huge dynamic hologram of the emperor Neo from Atlantis Legend (False Messiah) appeared in the sky and talks to all the world in the same time that they created human race to be their slaves(humans for Freemasons are animals that's why they insists and still in the documentaries that human origin is an Ape and is coming from evolution theory of Charles Darwin).

The emperor Neo ordered the world to surrender to his power or they will be destroyed completely and he showed them the Blue Beam Weapon light emerging from a Nazis design huge UFO to a satellite in the orbit. You see now that the Nazis UFOs are involved in this conspiracy.

This Blue Beam light was showed to the entire world that he destroyed part of Paris where The emperor appeared at first time and talked to the world.

Here I request from you to remember the talk of the Nazi engineer Wernher Von Braun to Doctor Carol Rosin who still alive until today about the weaponization of the space and I can confirm that It's a reality not a science fiction as they programmed us via their Hollywood movies and television series.

In the first draw below sequences showing a great Nazis UFO design from Haunebu models appears in the sky of Paris at 7 AM one of the walkers detected it in front of the Arc Of Triumph from the heart of Paris. Then the huge dynamic hologram of the emperor Neo appeared too.

The second draw shows the huge hologram talks to the people worldwide and threats them if they don't surrender they'll be killed. The huge dynamic hologram is present in more than a country and city in the same time. He talked in the same time with different languages and this is a miraculous technology!

The Dynamic Hologram Appeared In The Same Time In So Many Countries : UK, China, USA, Japan & Paris

The huge dynamic hologram of Neo showed the world people the blue beam light weapon and how it contacted two satellites in the orbit then hit Paris and destroyed a part of it. Remark here that they don't care about USA or Europe or UK and their citizens all these democracies are just temporary tools for them that's why they protects these democracies againt The military Coups as long as they need them to accomplish their agendas.

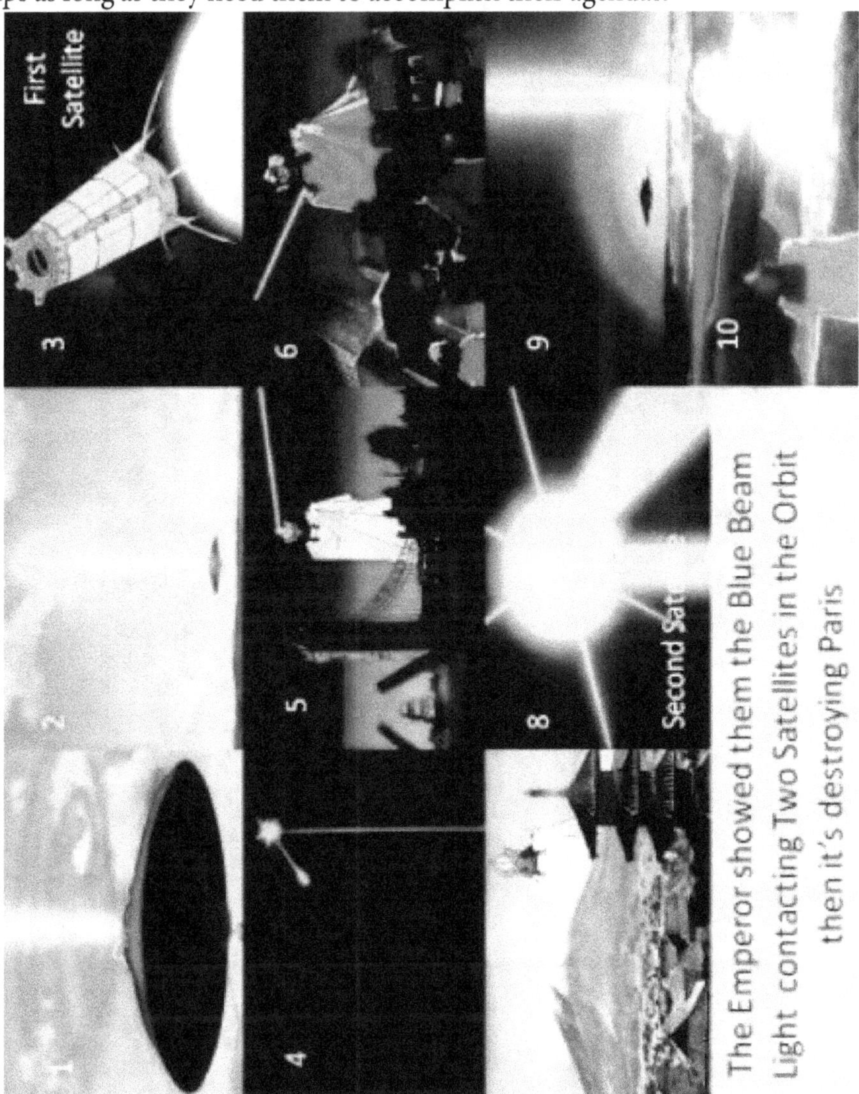

Another proof that The Nazis leaders or Army generals are from the high ranking Freemasonry grades and they work for the Freemasonry agendas and for the fake aliens invasion is a video recorded by a normal person showing a Nazi UFO lightning and drawing the eye of Egypt pyramid(The Freemasonry Eye) that we see in the US Dollar and this is another proof that Egypt is the final target and station for the Free masons and greater Israel project and this is a huge proof that the Nazis are involved in the blue beam project and sure other projects.

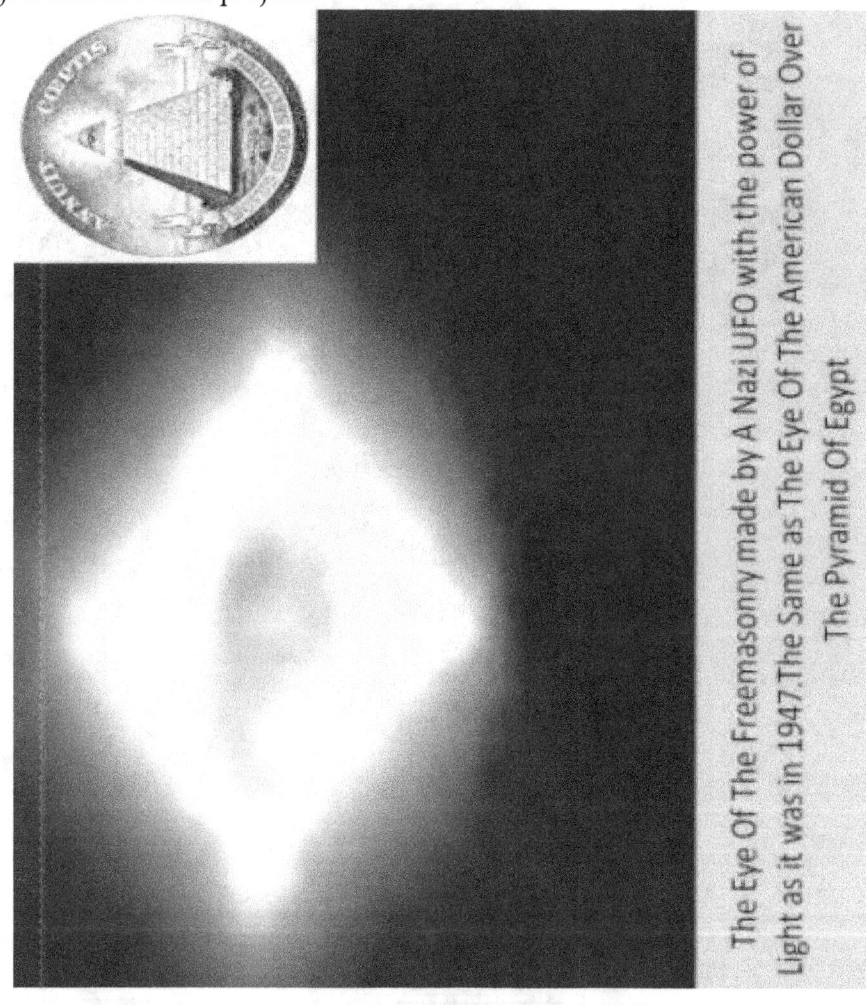

The Eye Of The Freemasonry made by A Nazi UFO with the power of Light as it was in 1947.The Same as The Eye Of The American Dollar Over The Pyramid Of Egypt

Another static hologram Freemasonry Eye sent over Russia in a cloudy day:

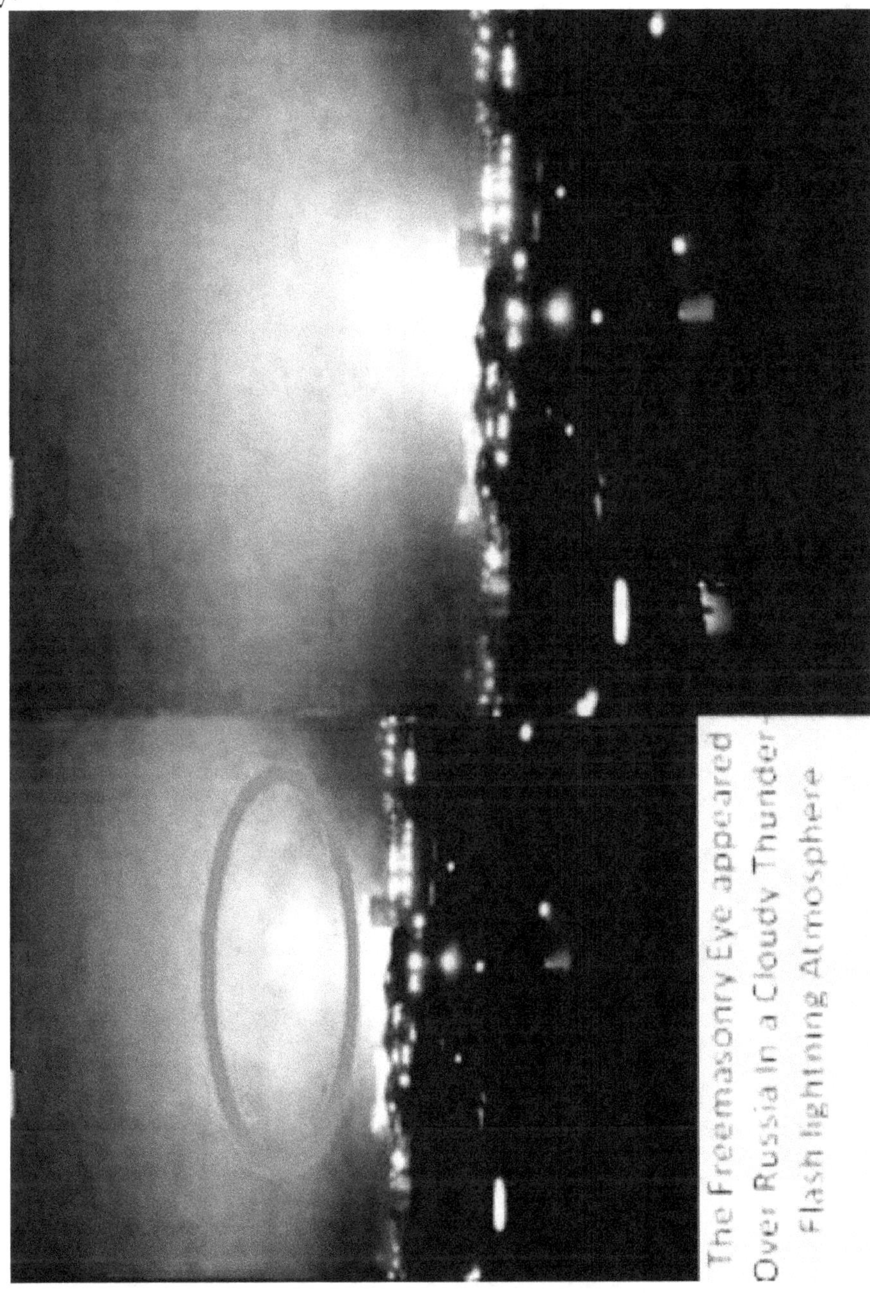

In Guadalajara Mexico The Freemasonry eye was formed by Nazis UFOs
:

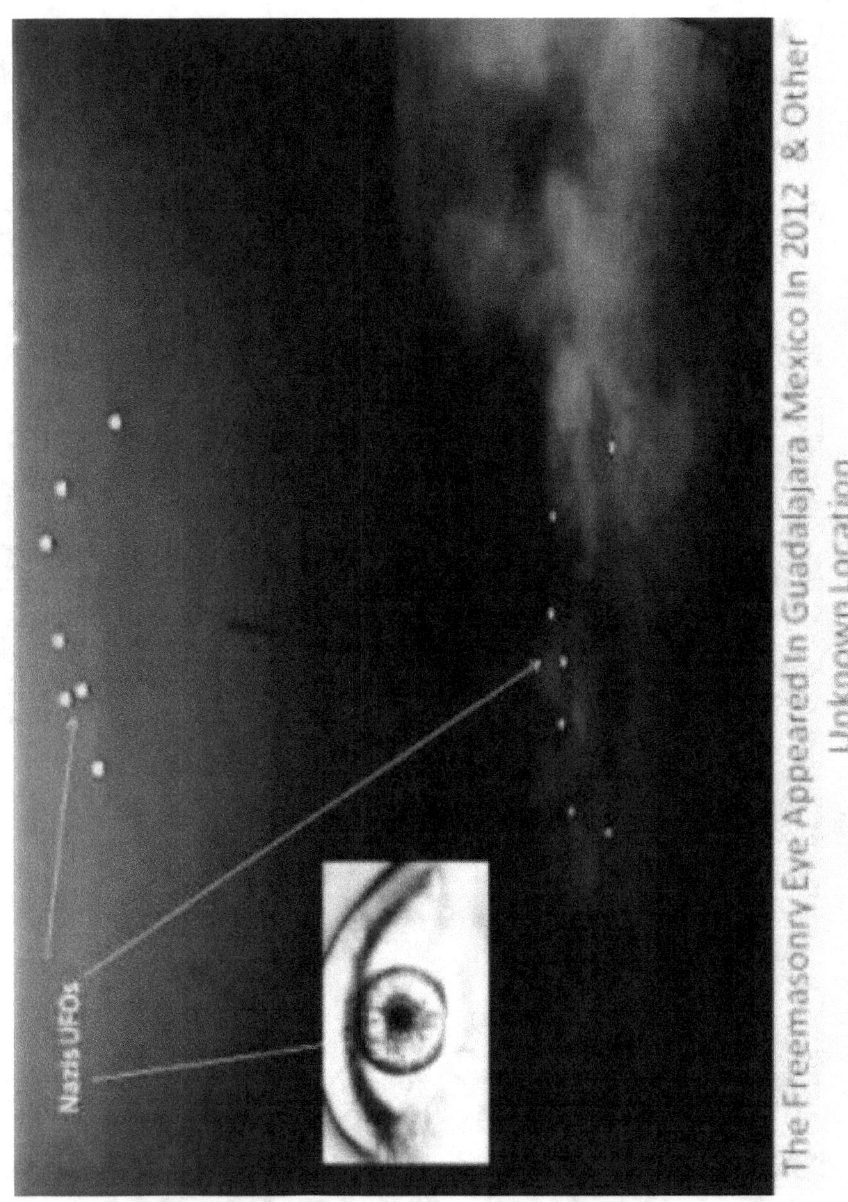

The Freemasonry Eye Appeared In Guadalajara Mexico In 2012 & Other Unknown Location

The pyramids and triangles belonging to Freemasonry theology were and still formed by Nazis UFOs worldwide to inform people with the subliminal message techniques programming their subconscious that they are under the Freemasonry Rule:

The Triangle As
The
Freemasonry
Pyramid Form

The Nazis send the same message which is the world is under the Freemasonry Rule and they are part of it via the movement of a Nazi UFO in front of The Freemasonry symbol the greatest obelisk in the world side by side with The White House in Washington DC and as we know all the presidents of United States stand up in front of this Obelisk the day of their inauguration some of them knows about the rule of Freemasonry but they don't have the complete image.

How did I knew the 500 millions of humans is the required number for greater Israel population? Simply by Georgia Guide Stone which has ten subliminal messages talking about the prosperity of the world and its sustainability with 8 different languages. For me those instructions are from the 33 degree freemasons to program people but none knows and imagine that and if they listen about that they'll consider it as a conspiracy theory no more! The ten guidelines which conforms the freemasonry speech to others when they talks about their vision to the world and this is real, the freemasons talks always about the phase after greater Israel kingdom is governing but when someone disobey it will be punished at that time they are disingenuous, deceptive and deceitful:

-Maintain humanity under 500,000,000 in perpetual balance with nature.

-Guide reproduction wisely, improving fitness and diversity.

-Unite humanity with a living new language.

-Rule passion, faith, tradition, and all things with tempered reason.

-Protect people and nations with fair laws and just courts.

-Let all nations rule internally resolving external disputes in a world court.

-Avoid petty laws and useless officials.

-Balance personal rights with social duties.

-Prize truth, beauty, love seeking harmony with the infinite.

-Be not a cancer on the Earth, Leave room for nature, Leave room for nature.

The Two Freemasonry Specificities The Lucifer Or Baphomet and God for them is mesurable and can be controlled that's Why they put its Name Between Compasses and a Square

Now how did I knew that the 33 degree Freemasons are children Of Israel and behind the blue beam project , simply via The Quran which is the only heaven religion holy book unchanged and not modified for 14 centuries, it's the same letter by letter. The Original Torah and Evangile the two holy books for Judaism and Christianity heaven religions are somewhere and they'll be reappeared at end times but what we have now are modified beside the Bible who is an assembly of old and new testaments from the 16th century done with my point of view by the 33 degree freemasons to make Christians believes in future in the Israel Kingdom story.

That's not means that we don't believe in all the material on these books , in the contrary we take from them but we take in consideration that there are changes made through centuries.

In the Quran the great control on earth by the 33 degree freemasons is mentioned in the chapter of: Al-issra(Night Journey) in the verse 4:

" And We conveyed to the Children of Israel in the Scripture(The Book): You will commit evil(Corruption) on earth twice, and you will rise to a great height."

Unfortunately, the translation is not loyal to the original Arabic version. Albert Pike the 33 degree freemasons was from children of Israel he wrote and updated the book "Morals and Dogma" which is the holy book for the Freemasonry followers they give this book starting from the third degree followers. The Strange point in this book, the 33 degree is not mentioned, we find the 32 degree as the last chapter! Why?

Because the 33 degree is dedicated only for the children of Israel. From my research in Freemasonry I found the 33 degree free masons must be descendants of Solomon who was king and prophet in the same time and other ones the most important they comes from Jacob or Israel the well known prophet who has 12 children including prophet Joseph peace and blessings be upon them all. Naturally, the prophets has no relation with the agenda made via the Babylon Talmud written by Infidel Rabbis in Babylon approximately 6000 years ago.

Those people are loyal to their ancestors agenda which making greater Israel Kingdom to worships the Satan instead of God again I confirm that the Judaism is a religion of God and never and ever she works against the faith of God on earth so Jews and Judaism has no relation with this agenda.

Muslims around the world discussed for decades the two evil or corruptions made by children of Israel mentioned in this verse and forget about the second part of this verse: the great high.

The great high is: The planet earth and the Solar system(the earth is flat with tens of continents not just 6 and majority of the aliens or extraterrestrials are from these far away continents the only way to attains these continents is with the technology of flying saucers with speed of 10000 km/hour and more: The Nazis and aliens technology that has long term breath in the contrary of combustion planes, ships and submarines except the nuclear ones) and the built of the humanity conscious after the world war 2 and presented it as an evolution in science space and astronomy despite majority were discovered centuries earlier if you see the constellations you'll find many are with Arabic names.

The vertical launch of rockets is too from the Nazis themselves when they hitted London with the new technology rockets in WWII the changing things are the designs and quantity of fuel used!

Why the planet earth and the solar system? Simply if you believe that you live in an earth as the center of universe (the universe structure is seven earth in the same level, every earth is related with a sky or a heaven, first earth with first sky, second earth with the second sky, until the seventh earth and sky every earth and sky connected with a mountain called : Kaf).

When you believe that you're the center of this universe you'll ask why ?You'll answer that we are very important in this universe and you'll believe really that God or Allah sent prophets to make you believe in him and do what he wants from you doing in your daily life(all the good things) so you'll be fidel and loyal to God on earth and try to be a good person and expect paradise after your death. This is against the 33 degree Freemasons will!

The second cause for implanting the planet earth and solar system ideas on the human heads is when you feel that you're nothing in this universe just a point of a Milky Way galaxy you'll accept easier the idea of an extraterrestrials existence and an aliens invasion to earth and this is what the Freemasons wants, off course beside the subliminal message technology by the Hollywood movies about the invasion, the television series, the documentaries, the daily news, etc.

The same concept is now used for the climate change big lie to depopulate earth with an ethical way without asking doubting questions. Punishing some countries with indirect manner if they are against their political or economic agendas as examples by destroying infrastructures with floods, storms and hurricanes and in the future they'll try to make famines by destroying cereals and they already did drought in so many areas worldwide. Climate change can never be in a huge world not closed sphere as they programmed us.

Before all this, it was and still the evolution theory by insisting that the origin of humans is Apes not from Adam and Eve to deny the existence of God and the story mentioned in the three heaven religions: Judaism, Christianity and Islam. They insists too about the unicellular world at first then pluri-cellulars then animals changing with time legs to wings and vice versa they do this with their mainstream media from kids cartoons to the movies and documentaries the strange thing people pays money to watch this, they make them stronger.

The starting great high on earth was felt when they invented the banking system by the Rothschild family in the seventieth century in Europe then to the world. Thanks to this huge amount of money they did and still doing all the mentioned points above.

In January 11th, 1907, a Hawaiian Gazette wrote that a flat earth map manuscript has been found inside a Copper Cylinder. This manuscript is regarded as a copy of the map that comes from a Buddhist Temple in the mountains of Central Japan. Doctor Kobayashi, a renowned Japanese physician and surgeon in Honolulu said that he had received a copy of a map believed to be created by Chinese imams 10 centuries ago (Imam in Islam is the person who leads the daily prayers on Mosque or the weekly prayer every Friday).

It was his brother who found this manuscript brought earlier by a monk who went to the mountains for the search of health healing. The manuscript contains Plain images with beautiful bow maps no book explains this geography it was in Fujiyama area where the beautiful blue sea is adorned with screens and canoes and strange images of Japanese women. Doctor

Kobayashi projected to write a novel about this manuscript but after a period of time nothing occurred and the doctor info are unknown.

The image below is from the manuscript aged with 10 centuries under it an approximate projection of the real world map. If we want to know the entire truth we need the technology of flying saucers not more to reach those far away continents, unfortunately the 33 degree freemasons succeeded to hold this technology for them to forbid people to know the hidden truth. But we should work on seriously.

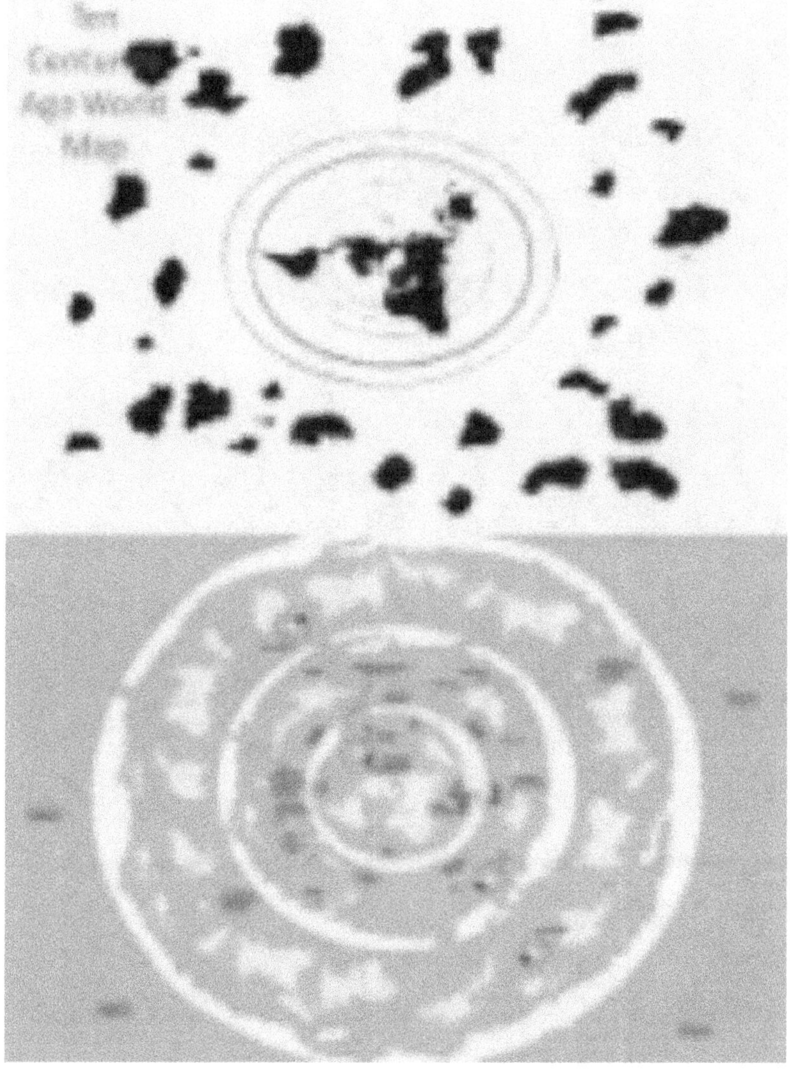

Don't miss out!

Visit the website below and you can sign up to receive emails whenever Mohamed Cherif publishes a new book. There's no charge and no obligation.

https://books2read.com/r/B-A-SXSU-ABRAC

Connecting independent readers to independent writers.

About the Author

Mohamed Cherif is a writer in different fields of knowledge, politics, and sciences. He has physics sciences master's degree. He writes in English and French languages. He has several books like Truth About Extraterrestrials, Hidden History of the Giants, Islam As You Never Knew, Blue Beam Project a Zionists-illuminatis Advanced Weapon for the 21 st Century. He is an environment Activist and supports Civil Societies and Anti-Tyranny movements around the world.